The Kingdom Culture Community

Taking It Back To Our Roots

Rev. Anthony Martin

20 Time Author-Inspirational/Motivational

Evangelistic Speaker

The Kingdom Culture Fellowship Ministries
& Christian Self Publishing Co.

Copyright © 2014 ~ 2020 by Rev. Anthony Martin

The Kingdom Culture Community
Taking It Back To Our Roots
By Rev. Anthony Martin
The 2nd Edition
Printed in the United States of America

ISBN 978-1-63273-015-2

All rights reserved solely by the author. The author guarantees all contents are original. No part of this book may be reproduced in any form without the permission of the author. The views expressed in this book are not necessarily all those of the publisher.

Unless otherwise indicated, Bible quotations are taken from
The Kingdom Culture Exploratory Study Bible
The Kingdom English Standard Bible.

The Kingdom Culture Fellowship Ministries
& Christian Self-Publishing Co.

www.thekingdomcultureblog.com

This Book is dedicated to:

The Men & Woman that entered in my life
The Patriarch, Ted Wilson (Grand Dad) Before the Lord
The Matriarch, Lucille K. Wilson (Grandma); before the Lord
The Instructor, William L. Martin (Father) in our Midst
The Teacher, Gwendolyn Martin (Mother); before the Lord
The Student, Taylor D. Lincoln (Daughter)

The most inspiring Men that entered in my life:

The Almighty GOD (The Father)

The Lord and Savior Jesus Christ (The Messiah)

The Holy Spirit (The Comforter)

The President of the United States Barack H. Obama

My Spiritual Overseer, Pastor Anthony E. Moore (Caroline Missionary Baptist Church)

My Spiritual Overseer, Pastor Kenneth Spears (Cornerstone COGIC)

My Spiritual Father, Asst. Pastor Lee B. Gaston (Cornerstone COGIC)

My Spiritual Mentors Dr. Myles Munroe (BFMMM)

Dr. Tony Evans (The Urban Alternative)

Dr. John T. Rhodes (Trinity Baptist Church

Dr. John Maxwell (Best Selling Author)

Ralph Marston (Inspirational Motivator)

Earl "Pop" Riddick Sr. (A Father)

Ben "Daddy" Franklin (A Father)

Harold "Daddy" Ligon (Toast) (A Father)

Matt "Pop" Owens (A Father)

Sylvester "Elder" Norville (A Father)

To My Family Friends & Neighbors

Contents

The Preface	iii
The Review	vii
Introduction	viii

Part I: GODS Family Structure

1. The Head (Foundation), The Man and The Husband ..	11
2. The Helpmeet, The Woman and The Wife	35
3. The Child, The Teen and The Adult	51
4. The Purpose for Sex	72
5. The Purpose for the Family	83

Part II: GODS Foundation

6. 600 Million	95
7. Why are you here?	98
8. The Priest of the Home	103
9. The Inheritance	115
A Message to the Family	
The Author	

The Kingdom Culture Fellowship Ministries & Christian Self Publishing Co.

The Review

Rev. Anthony Martin breaks down the biblical meaning of family, from the Old Testament through to the New Testament and shows how understanding the family unit relates to living in this world as citizens of the Kingdom of God. This stirring and compelling book will surprise readers who think they have heard all they need to know about Christianity, the nuclear family and the larger church family.

- *The opening content of the book (Introduction and Chapter 1) is a very effective launch pad for the book. Readers will immediately become engaged in the content through learning something new about what "family" really meant in the scriptures. From giving them something new to diving into personal testimony, the opening pages will definitely capture and hold readers' attention, which gives the book a lot of potential.*
- *The author crafted his discussion very efficiently in that he chose just the right words to show the connection between God's design and our daily lives. Many people, even baptized Christians and regular churchgoers, have a very hard time making connections between spiritual principles and their every day experiences. Readers will definitely have many "aha" moments thanks to the author's stellar message.*
- *The entire book is replete with references to Bible verses, which shows all readers, whether they have been walking with the Lord for many years or know nothing about Him, that this book is 100% based on God Himself, not any opinion, religion, movement, or other source of inspiration. The author's motive clearly is to be used as God's instrument to communicate to His beloved children.*

INTRODUCTION

The basic household unit provides a person's central relationships, nurture, and support. The basic composition of a family changes from the Old Testament to the New Testament. Therefore, the search for the traditional biblical family is difficult. However, the search is important to understand the essential family structures, relationships, commitments, and functions. Jesus Christ, along with the New Testament writers, used family images to describe the nature of faith and the church. Understanding the biblical definition of family can serve as a guide for living out faith in the family more effectively. The biblical portrayal of family represents the basic structures and foundations of the Near East during biblical times, conditions that still prevail over much of the East today. Throughout biblical times the structures and relationships changed. Likewise, the commitments and functions changed. The span of the Old Testament allowed for a lot of transition in the family. Their understanding of the nature of God as well as their culture influenced much of the Hebrew family life. The Old Testament family represents a larger body that the English word suggests. There are two Hebrew words that are used to refer to the family. One word, *mishpachah*, was used to describe the larger patriarchal clan, which included those persons related by blood, marriage, slave ship, and even animals (as found in the fourth commandment in Exodus). Occasionally even strangers or sojourners could be included in the larger household. The second word, *bayith*, was used to suggest the place of residence or household. It had multiple meanings. It represented a clan of descendants (Genesis 18:19), or property and persons of a particular place or residence on which and on whom one depended (Job 8:15).Central to this household was the oldest male relative, who was viewed as the "father", master, and ultimate authority, thus signifying the family as the father's house. All who belonged to him and claimed their allegiance to him were considered part of the household and were similar in beliefs and values. In Genesis 7:1 Noah and his household were directed to enter the ark. Beyond the household were the larger clan, the tribe, and the nation, which were descendants of Abraham, from which the people of Israel originated. Relationships with the oldest male placed him as the center of the household. He was expected to marry and often have more than one wife (Genesis 38:8-10; Deuteronomy 25:5-10). Though monogamy was widely practiced in Israel, polygamy was common.

The Kingdom Culture Community

Abraham, Jacob, and David were all husbands of more than one wife, and they also had concubines, who had a lower status than a wife (Genesis 46:26). The creation of Adam and Eve was a model of the monogamous relationship of one male and one female, as were many other couples in the Bible (Genesis 1-2). The authority of the father was quite significant, even though he may actually have been the grandfather or great-grandfather. His responsibilities included begetting, instructing, disciplining, and nurturing. Abraham had the power to sacrifice his son (Genesis 22:1). The father could even destroy family members if they enticed him from his loyalty to God (Deuteronomy 13:6-10). However, the father was also to love and the divine mercy of the New Testament was based on the compassionate Old Testament father (Psalm 103:1). The function of the family in the New Testament was secondary to the primary purpose of the family of God. Obedience to Christ and doing God's will was the calling for everyone. This faith commitment, then, shaped the purpose and function of the family. Christ-like love guided the family and the purpose of the family was to give witness to the love of God and bring people to a saving relationship with God through Jesus Christ, thus creating the larger family of God. The purpose for this book is to bring the awareness level of "The Kingdom Culture" of GOD back to the for-front of the life of GOD'S people. The family of GOD has been reduced from being citizens of the Kingdom of GOD to being Christians. This terminology seems to lower the standards of GOD'S way of life on earth as it is in Heaven. We as a Christian community allow many leniencies, which seem to weaken the Law of GOD. This is why many so called Christians do not read the Bible, because the Bible demands that you do and many don't care to do that which GOD put in them to do. The principle reason for this book is to show the purpose of how things work through the wisdom of GOD in knowing how to "LIVE GOD'S KINGDOM CULTURE".

PART I

GODS

FAMILY

STRUCTURE

CHAPTER I

The Head (Foundation), The Man, The Husband

Gen. 1: 26-28...Says...Then God said, "Let us make man in our image, in our likeness, and let them rule over the fish of the sea and the birds of the air, over all livestock, over all the earth, and over all the creatures that moves along the ground," So God created man in his own image, in the image of God he created him; male and female he created them. God blessed them and said to them, "Be fruitful and increase in number; fill the earth and subdue it. Rule over the fish of the sea and birds of the air and over every living creature that moves on the ground." Gen. 2: 15-18... The Lord God took the man and put him in the Garden of Eden to work it and take care of it. And the Lord God commanded the man, "You are free to eat from any tree in the garden; but you must not eat from the tree of knowledge of good and evil, for when you eat of it you will surely die." The Lord God said, "It is not good for the man to be alone. I will make a helper suitable for him. 1 Cor. 9:3 Now I want you to realize that the Head of every man is Christ, and the Head of every woman is man, and the Head of Christ is God. Before the fall of Adam and Eve God set the stage for them in the Garden of Eden in perfect form and atmosphere. In the Garden there was perfect peace in the family setting; Adam was given authority over the earth and in Adams authority notice in scripture God created Adam as a man and not a child or a boy because a child or a boy would not fit in such an atmosphere of authority. Only a man given authority by God would fit such a hierarchy position, now there are five things God gave Adam 1.)Eden..... 2.) Work..... 3.) Cultivation..... 4.) Protection..... 5.) Gods Command but there is five things God did first with male and that is 1.) The first human God created was the male, 2.) The first thing God gave the male was his image, 3.) The first place God place the male was in the Garden of Eden, 4.) The first assignment God gave the male was work, 5.) The first instruction God gave the male was cultivate.

Many of us coming up looking at scripture, believed that the first thing GOD gave the male was dominion over the earth, this is misinformation and has been the bases of the down fall of man's position and relationship on earth, is this attitude of authority first. If you study the scriptures more carefully you would discover that the first thing God decided was not how much power and authority man was going to have, the first thing God decided was man's identity and What is man's identity? "THE IMAGE OF GOD." See, the bible says...God foreknew all things long before the foundation of the world because he planned these things; God set the things of the world up according to his purpose and plan, which means good and evil. And the one thing God knew is that man had to be tested as his greatest project, we all were destined to be tested. Our first point of testing would be who we are and what our purpose on earth is and Adam being first man (after the pre-Adamite world) he was first in line for this powerful testing of man's will. So God put in order all the things that would be man's first point of attack, in doing so God gave man the good of all things first (Heaven) over the evil of all things (Hell), this in the manner of the perfect world before the fall. This also accounts to that in the perfect world one difference between the Kingdom of God and the kingdom Devil is that God presents Heaven from beginning to end (Alpha & Omega) and Devils kingdom don't exist, but because of the fall the difference is now that Devil presents Heaven first Hell last and God presents Hell first and Heaven last. So it was vitally important for God to give image (Identity) first because the greatest destruction to a man's life is not knowing "Who he is" or "What his purpose is" on this earth, that is the greatest tragedy to "MAN." It does not matter how much money you have, what position you carry in life, how much power and authority you possess, if you don't know who you are as a man you are dangerous in a world of death and destruction and you will easily add to this world of death and destruction.

The Head (Foundation), The Man, The Husband

Here is what we missed in this matter of God's purpose and plan in our lives, we keep thinking it is dominion or ruler ship with an iron fist over the earth and in all that we are too have, we have been chasing "Power over Purpose", believing that our purpose here on earth was and is to obtain power, man was created to rule and dominate the earth,...Yes! But the first thing given to man was not power, it was image. See! God knew that power would be in trouble if image was not in order, why because the fall of man would give devil the power over man to redirect man's image of God to the image of the world. This is the reason why we will never be satisfied with having more money, you don't need money first "MEN," money is attracted to the right self-image, money moves toward a man who knows who he is and when you know who you are you don't seek to obtain power by way of having more money. Solomon says, in (Eccl. 5:10-12) He who loves money will not be satisfied with money, nor he who loves abundance with its income. This too is a waste. When good things increase, those who consume them increase. So what is the advantage to their owners except to look on? The sleep of the working man is pleasant, whether he eats little or much; but the full stomach of the rich man does not allow him to sleep. You can easily tell when a man has a low self-image; he has an inferiority complex, he looks to scheme or scam for things, so he needs to accumulate things to build up his insecurity that's why he has a lot of material things because he has no self-image and his identity is defined by what he has. A man who loses everything and still smile is a righteous man, a righteous man don't need things to be of value, because a righteous man give value too things. So God put in place the work, given Adam responsibility to go along with His Image because image needs a place of existence and when God places something in us it must be express in the world, so as Adam is placed in the Garden, Gods image was there to be express. We must know and understand that your work is not your job. When God place Adam in the Garden He gave Adam dominion over it and everything in it, so noted everything including the woman. Now everything means five different kingdoms on earth, 1.) Fish....2.), Birds....3.), Livestock....4.), All the Earth, plants, trees, grass....and 5.), everything that creeps on the ground (insects). Now your job is your skill, a policeman, a fireman and a postman that's one skill, your work is the gift that you were born with.

The Kingdom Culture Community

For instants when you go to your job you enter in an atmosphere of people all operating on one skill and in that skill you put in an 8 hour day and you has a human person over you called a boss. When you do the wrong thing on this job you are fired from this job. When you are fired from this job you "MAN"….go home to your place of rest and you are met at the door by your wife and she says "hello honey I have work for you to do, I need you to cut the grass, I need you to fix the roof, I need you to too wash the car, I need you to clean the basement. Now take your job and your work at home and line it up to the Garden Adam was given dominion over and see which one is identical to the Garden before the fall, "THE HOME" because in the home you "MAN," have dominion over the work which is your gift you were born with, your job which is your skill and have a human boss over you are not identified with the Garden. God did not place any one over Adam, this is why we men naturally hate to be ruled over because we were not created to be ruled, but created to dominate. Only after the fall is when God place in the Garden a Guardian Angel to protect the tree of life in the east of the Garden and this Angel was used to fire Adam and Eve from the Garden…"A BOSS"….see the Identity. "YOUR JOB IS NOT THE WORK GOD GAVE YOU MEN" It is important to know the different so you can know your purpose, other than that you will be stuck in a place that you hate. The one thing that we have to understand as men is simply knowing GOD did not create man to rule man, GOD never said to man have dominion over man, it was the woman, the animal kingdoms and the earth that was given to us to rule and regulate. This is why we as men have many issues on the job and other control environments simply because we were not made to be controlled but too control all things on earth, by way of GOD's Kingdom plan and purpose in our life on this place called earth. We must know and understand that we only can rule our own GOD given territory, which then we collaborate that portion of our dominion over the earth. To rule over or have dominion over this place such as the earth means all that the earth gives off in trouble, difficulty, problems, issues, pain and agony is for man to put in check or in perspective that these things be resolve as they come, not man singular, man collectively Paul says— "We should no longer be children, tossed to and fro and carried about with every wind of doctrine."

The Head (Foundation), The Man, The Husband

He added, "But, speaking the truth in love, may we grow up in all things into Him who is the head— Christ— from whom the whole body, joined and knit together by what every joint supplies, according to the effective working by which every part does its share, causes growth of the body for the edifying of itself in love" (Eph. 4:14-16). Our dominion was not given to us singular it was given to us as a whole, in a collaborative collective bargaining reason and relationship as men in Christ. We are given a limited time to carry out GOD's purpose here on earth and the time that you think you have is not set up for your foolishness or ill gotten ways. What you may believe to be correct could very well be a waste of time given to do the purpose that you don't have a clue to which you must carry out. Many men believe there job is there purpose or just doing a good deed holds as your purpose, your purpose is that what you are born with, and do you know what's in you? Do you know GOD well enough to know what you're here for? Do you understand the struggle you've come through? Do you understand struggle at all? Or more so "DO YOU KNOW GOD?" No matter whom you are or where you come from every one of us has been given unique purpose we all were born with. GOD created every one of us with this unique gift to make an impact on earth that it would be a lasting impact for generations to come, your impact as man on earth is to maintain the set stage Christ set for us from the foundations of the earth as Paul says— "Just as He chose us in Him before the foundation of the world, that we would be holy and blameless before Him" (Eph.1:4). Long before the world was established GOD chose us, we men, were given the position to govern this earth in accord to GODs purpose and plan place in us, not according to our ways and means. We are given the position to carry out the very assignment that is uniquely place in us that we specifically exercise our skill set for the very purpose of being a threat too devils kingdom, given devil no breathing room to take charge of our families, friends and neighbors. We should act as an legion of warriors daily simply because of devils legion of demons that stay on the war path twenty-four hours a day as he spoke to GOD when ask in Job— " The Lord ask Satan, "where have you come from? "Satan answered the Lord, "from wandering all over the earth." Job 1:7; other Hebrew writings speak extensively in saying— "looking to devour man all over the earth," in other words we men are under constant attack to remove us from whom

GOD placed on this earth to be "Manager" of this place called earth, we are to maintain our families, our communities our environment that all that is in it live with honor, respect and glory first too GOD and then by way of his image we live. We cannot continue this easy path of destruction that many of you are on, given devil an open door policy to do what he wish in your life, leading you away from being men and developing your choices to be like "WOMEN" through a "LIE" of homosexual lifestyle. Given Satan the keys to death over your life when GOD through His son Christ Jesus upon dying on the cross and descending down into hell and taking the keys of death from the hands of Satan and making death a footstool under His feet. We no longer have to fall under death simply because death is under our feet as Paul says— "even when we were dead in our transgressions, made us alive together with Christ (by grace you have been saved), and raised us up with Him, and seated us with Him in the heavenly places in Christ Jesus…. (Eph. 2:6-7). In a world of trouble and chaos, in which we as men brought about such foolishness by way of allowing ourselves to be tossed to and fro like the wind, when we have no business in such turmoil being the very ones given dominion over the earth. We have a God given duty to act in accord to the will of God, in His image to stand as the foundation of the family place in our care under our instruction by way of one wife and respectful children. Our nature is too follow the life of God as we were created for, not too follow our own desires but that which represent God and that which represent God is that which we were made in, His "IMAGE." God's image represents a unified body called the "Trinity" a bond that will never be broken under no circumstances. This is the same standard God holds man too under no circumstance man should be apart from God, under no circumstances should man be apart from a wife, under no circumstances should man be apart from his children, this is not what God has given us dominion to become, independent men from our families. We are the bond to hold us together in Christ; we hold the most important position on earth in which we are held to a strict account to manage this earth accordingly as Christ by way of the instructions of the Holy Spirit. Too many men are given up their position as men in a world you were given strict instructions to manage, along with the knowledge, understanding and wisdom to do so, how do you give up such a position over the "WORLD."

The Head (Foundation), The Man, The Husband

It is simple when you have no idea of what you are, who you are or why you even exist, you have no position to hold on too, How can you hold to a position you never knew you possess. This is why the bible shows us Gods purpose and plan will go on with us or without us. The word of God tells us that God will supply our needs and all that we receive is nothing but supplies, the problem behind that is we take the supplies and use the supplies for ourselves on earth but our treasures and rewards are stored in Heaven. We are taking our supplies and using them in the manner of our treasures and rewards and Christ says we already then have received our reward on earth that we were to receive in Heaven. The Greatest tool the devil use against us as men of God is independency, if Satan can cause us to be independent from God he then can have his way, and fallen astray means fallen prey to "Death." Having dominion over the earth comes with our will to choose outside of God's control of that area of our life, so in doing so we don't give God the experience of what we experience at the moment of our lives in our experiences, How? By not choosing him to intervene in our experiences, How do you choose? By prayer and the spoken word (Sanctification), many times we think God test us for discipline reason in what we do and in many cases that's true but in other cases God test us men not on what we do but for what we know. This is why we as men must always depend on God, case in point, radio test their systems for dependency on their back up in case something goes wrong same with TV Station, in other words God test us in two forms "A manner of Discipline" and " a manner of Dependency" or Faith. Who you love? Do you love the things that God gave or do you love God for what He has given you, that "Thing." These are the many of issues we face as men in going forth in God, one problem to note we have as men of God is many of you continue to try to prove your point in your life, instead of proving Gods point in your life, and you stop trying to prove your point and seek God's point then the righteous point will be made. We all need to understand our relationship with God and how that relationship dictates the man we will, or will not, be, we must learn how to discern the voice of the Lord through the instructions of the Holy Spirit and how to respond to that small still voice.

The Kingdom Culture Community

It is that very voice of love, mercy and kindness that we can somehow find ourselves at odds with when we are tempted, we as men need convictions that doesn't come from other men, we need convictions from hearing the voice of the Lord. They come from having a holy fear of God and knowing in your heart of hearts His will for you. Convictions allow a man to steady his walk in order to stay on the narrow road that leads to life, to be able to hear the voice of the Lord, discern his will in your life, and to act upon it in a way that brings him glory is everything you need to be a true man. OFF AND ON, As Paul says to the Ephesians, "Praise be to God and father of our lord Jesus Christ, Who has blessed us in the heavenly realms with every spiritual blessing in Christ. For he chose us in him before the creation of the world to be holy and blameless in the sight of Him, (Eph. 1:3-4), then he added, "You were taught, with regard to your former way of life, to put off your old self, which is being corrupted by its deceitful desires; to be made new in the attitude of your minds; and to put on the attitude of your minds; and to put on the new self, created to be like God in His true righteousness and holiness"— Eph. 4:21-24. How can we—creatures who are physical and spiritual and fallen in our sin—obey this verse? How can we triumph over our sin and our flesh to perform this profoundly spiritual act? More to the point the bible, if you and I have a hard enough time trying to obey this verse, how can immature men accomplish this? Simple every immature unrighteous man will have the same origin as every one of the righteous spiritual victories. To rise above the temptations of the world you must set the mind on the things of the Spirit. Scripture teaches us to put to death those thoughts and desires that are of the earthly nature and to begin to show evidence of our new spiritual nature that is "being renewed in knowledge in the image of God. Put to death, therefore, whatever belongs to your earthly nature: sexual immorality, impurity, lust, evil desires and greed, which is idolatry, because of these; the wrath of God is coming? You used to walk in these ways, in the life you once lived, but now you must rid yourselves of all such things as anger, rage, malice, slander, and filthy language from your lips. Do not lie to each other, since you have taken off your old self with its practices and have put on the new self, which is being renewed in knowledge in the image of God. Here there is no Greek or Jew, circumcised or uncircumcised, barbarian, Scythian, slave or free, but Christ is all, and is in all.

The Head (Foundation), The Man, The Husband

Therefore, as God's chosen people, holy and dearly loved, clothe yourselves with compassion, kindness, humility, gentleness and patience. Bear with each other and forgive whatever grievances you may have against one another, forgive as the Lord forgave you, and over all these virtues put on love, which binds them all together in perfect unity. (Col. 3:5-14). We have been made in God's image, we have the amazing privilege of being spiritual beings, just as God is a spiritual being, the responsibility that comes with that privilege (privilege and together) is that we are called to pursue spiritual growth. We are called to become ever more "like God in true righteousness and holiness." This pursuit is the essence of honorable manhood, even honorable young manhood. That's a daunting project, isn't it? Does it seem impossible? As impossible, I don't know, a camel squeezing through the eye of a needle? If that's how you see it, you're on the right track. Not only that, but you're in the right place to be able to communicate this truth accurately to the young men, for our Savior told us that, "with man this is impossible, but with God all things are possible" (Matt 19:26). Here's the challenge men need to understand, like Adam, we are required to be perfectly blameless and completely holy in our obedience to God. The problem, of course, is that none of us ever do this perfectly, as James said, "We all stumble in many ways" (James 3:2), so if we are sure to fail from time to time, yet God calls us to be perfectly holy, what does it mean to walk as a man before God? It means that we must put our trust completely in the finished work of Jesus Christ, who alone can make us holy and pure. It means that when we stumble and fall short of the glory of God we do two things, First, we return to the Lord and ask him for forgiveness, genuinely repentant yet confident that this specific sin we just committed was a sin Christ died to forgive. Second, we pick ourselves up again and keep going, continually seeking to obey God by the power of his grace. This is the basis of all repentance: turning away from our sin and in our love of God heading in the opposite direction, back to him again and again. This is where our degree of familiarity and our current experience with God's word becomes crucial. Through the Bible we learn and are reminded of what God commands of us, and we recall the power and love and grace he offers us for both obedience and forgiveness.

This means we should be continually growing in our knowledge of God through his word, the Psalmist certainly got it right when he wrote, "How can a young man keep his way pure? By living according to your Word, I seek you with all my heart; do not let me stray from your commands, I have hidden your Word in my heart that I might not sin against you" (Psalm 119:9-11).

Manhood

So then, are spiritual creatures, we are made in God's image, we are called by his grace to live in perfect holiness before him, and when we fail we can look to Christ for forgiveness and fresh grace. How then can we measure our progress, our success? How can we know we are becoming more like God in righteousness and true holiness? Actually, it's not that difficult, as we growth can be readily seen in the virtues, or character traits, that rise to the surface, what virtues should we aim for? What do we want our sons to be like? Let's start with a definition of manhood that is currently popular in much of western culture. According to this definition, a "real man" can be described something like this: Muscular and athletic, Never overweight, Definitely not an acne sufferer, A rugged individualist who answers only to himself, a person who is tolerant of everyone and everything, because there are no absolutes in his life, only opinions, open to many views of morality, truth, and right and wrong, a ladies' man, with the emphasis on the plural, even if his choice in "ladies" is another man, Basically deserving of anything he might want or desire, focused on being (or at least appearing to be) wealthy, smart, accepted, talented, liked, and admired. Is this the kind of man you hope your boy will become? Are these the "virtues" you want to see manifested in his life? I don't think so. In Galatians 5:19-21 Paul describes the nature to lead us into "sexual immorality, impurity and witchcraft; hatred, discord, jealousy, fits of rage, selfish ambition, dissensions, factions and envy; drunkenness, orgies, and the like." Paul then contrasts these detestable things of our sinful nature with the fruit of the Spirit of God in Gal. 5;22-23, "but the fruit of the Spirit is love, joy, peace, patience, kindness, goodness, faithfulness, gentleness and self-control." I believe we can distill from Scripture six virtues to use as benchmarks and goals, things we can hold onto, measures, evaluate, and work to improve as we mature.

The Head (Foundation), The Man, The Husband

It is not my intention to make an airtight case for these six being the only possible choices; certainly there are other virtues that can be identified in Scripture. My goal here — especially as you prepare to talk with your son—is to keep it simple by providing a biblically solid list that is easy to remember and will point your son in right direction. A biblical description of a real man is a follows. A real man is: Humble, Courageous, Morally Pure, Faithful, Selfless, and Self-Controlled. How well do these terms line up with that first set of bullet point—the worldly view of a man? Not a lot of overlap, is there? Where are the self-centeredness, self-seeking, and self-glorification that the world continually emphasizes? Where are the themes of consumption and indulgence? Where is the sense of entitlement? In their place, we see a striking emphasis on looking outward. The second set of bullet points describe a man who takes the attitude of a servant toward others, whose life is focused not on self-exaltation but on glorifying God with his life. The world's version of a man essentially sees others as raw material for his own gratification and glorification, the true man, on the other hand, according to God's definition, seeks to love his neighbor and to consider others as better than him. The Virtues of Men, these virtues are spiritual fruit, closely and directly associated with being like God in true righteousness and holiness, the more we become like God, the more these virtues will be evident in us. For each virtue there is a short definition and a few verses for emphasis and elaboration, paying close attention to these virtues will help you set your sights on exactly where you want to lead your son. Humility, to pursue humility means choosing to accept the fact that your knowledge and abilities are limited, and in light of that, you are regularly seeking help and graciously receiving advice and correction. This one is esteem: he who is humble and contrite in spirit, and trembles at my word (Isa. 66:2), all of you, clothe yourselves with humility toward one another, because, God opposes the proud but gives grace to the humble (1 Peter 5:8), Humility and the fear of the Lord bring wealth and honor and life (Prov. 22:4). Courage, to pursue courage means choosing to do what is right despite the opposition of others or of your own desires (often the more difficult enemy to fight), be on your guard; stand firm in the faith; be men of courage; be strong (1 Corinth. 16:13), so keep up your courage, men, for I have faith in God that it will happen just as he told me (Acts 27:25), Act with courage, and may the Lord be with those who do well, (2 Chronicles 19:11), Purity, to pursue moral purity means choosing to live by the highest moral principles in both speech and physical relations, despite your own desires to do otherwise, and despite any external pressure to compromise. How can a young man keep his way pure? By living according to your word (Psalm 119:9) treat younger men as brothers, older women as mothers, and younger women as sisters, with absolute purity (1 Tim. 5:1-2). Set an example for the believers in speech, in life, in love, in faith and in purity (1 Tim. 4:12), do not be hasty in the laying on of hands, and do not share in the sins of others, keep yourself pure (1 Tim. 5:22). Faithfulness., to pursue faithfulness means acting in integrity, keeping your words, and doing what is right before God, with fortitude and without complaint, because you trust God to give you the ability to complete all he has given you to do, so then, men ought to regard us as servants of Christ and as those entrusted with the secret things of God. Now it is required that those who have given a trust must prove faithful (1 Corinthians 4:1-2), Love the LORD, all his saints! The LORD preserves the faithful, but the proud he pays back in full. Be strong and take heart, all you who hope in the LORD (Psalm 31:23-24), A faithful man will be richly blessed (Prov. 28:20).

Selflessness, to pursue selflessness means placing the well-being of others before your own needs and desires. An unfriendly man pursues selfish ends; he defies all sound judgment (Prov. 18:1), Do nothing out of selfish ambition or vain conceit, but in humility consider others better than yourselves, Each of you should look not only to your own interest, but also to the interests of others (Philippians 2:2-4).For where you have envy and selfish ambition, there you find disorder and every evil practice (James 3:16). Self-control, to pursue self-control means to live according to the Spirit of God, choosing to glorify God with our lives and deny the sinful nature when tempted to do otherwise. Be self-controlled and alert, your enemy the devil prowls around like a roaring lion looking for someone to devour (1 Peter 5:8), Like a city whose walls are broken down is a man who lacks self-control (Prov. 25:28). But the fruit of the Spirit is love, joy, peace, patience, kindness, goodness, faithfulness, gentleness and self-control, against such things there is no law (Galatians 5:22-23).

The Head (Foundation), The Man, The Husband

We all need help, when society settles on a false definition of what is good and desirable in a man, the streets become full of males who have never grown into Biblical manhood. Guys like these might look cool, but morally they may be little more than children, what a sad and traffic things that so many boys today fall into this trap and never get out! They buy into the world's definition of manhood and end up going to their graves morally stunted. The externals of chasing this worldly definition of manhood—things like sexual conquests, shiny never qualify anyone for true manhood. Your son doesn't have to become a man like that, he has you to help him, and you have Christ, the Word of God, and fellow believers to help you. The truth is that we all need help, being a man is a daunting task, impossible on your own, to become more like Christ in true righteousness and holiness, a man's mind must be renewed and his heart must be regenerated. In short, your son needs divine intervention, and you must remind him of his dependence on God and the regenerating work of Jesus Christ. For your son to be the man that he was created to be requires full and complete reliance on Jesus Christ, It is in this God– given, God-empowered virtues that your talk with your son should be wrapped. I guarantee these are not character traits or choices that have been discussed with your son at a public school, They are rarely seen on television or in the movies, if you want to be sure your son has an understanding of what it means to be a man, you will most likely need to be the one to tell him. In any event, you are far and away the best one to tell him. The bibles says— as a man thinks within himself, so he is….(Prov. 23:7), if you think yourself to be less than a man you are, if anyone put the thought of any death disease in your thinking and you accept it than it will be, if you think you can't stand up against life's issues, than it will be, if you think you can't handle life's struggles, then you can't, if you think you can't handle life's difficulties then you won't, if you think you can't handle life's problems then so it will be. What was the purpose of all that struggle you came thru life for? What did you experience all that pain in life for? You weren't born without reason! God did not give purpose to all of creation to follow and live by and not give you a purpose. When Eve committed the sin in the Garden of Eden the bible says Adam was right there with her as she committed the sin, but the bible also says when God entered into the Garden through his son Christ Jesus (Lord) it was not Eve that was sought after, it was Adam that was sought after, Why? Simply because Adam was given the authority over the earth and everything in it, also it was Adam that was given the instructions to carry out the duties in which the garden was to be cared for and past down to Eve to do the same has her husband. When the things of this earth goes against us, when stuff fall apart in the families, when the community become disarray, when the church is not making an impact on the community as it should, when the kids are out of order, when the wife no longer set her eyes for you only, when the house is no longer a home. Who is the blame Devil? A defeated Foe? The bible says— "How you have fallen from heaven, morning star, son of the dawn! You have been cast down to the dawn! You have been cast down to the earth, you who once laid low the nations!......Those who see you stare at you, they ponder your fate: " Is this the man who shook the earth and made kingdoms tremble, the man who made the world a wilderness, who overthrow its cities and would not let his captives go home? (Isaiah 14:12 –23). He is a "DEFEATED FOE" so you can't put nothing on devil men, all things is based on our will to choose, that's the freedom the bible is clear about a man's responsibility to exercise spiritual maturity and spiritual leadership. Of course, this spiritual maturity takes time to develop, and it is a gift of the Holy Spirit working within the life of the believer, the disciplines of the Christian life, including prayer and serious Bible study, are among the means God uses to mold a boy into a man and to bring spiritual maturity into life of one who charged to lead a wife and family. Embrace maturity, as you may have heard it said: Maturity does not come with age, but with the acceptance of responsibility, if we are going to grow as men, we have to take full responsibility for our lives- blaming no one; owning our decisions; and deciding to grow and change- no matter what has come our way. Gen. 3:12 says— "after sinning, Adam said to God, "The woman whom you have given to me, she gave me of the tree and I ate." Notice how Adam dealt with his being caught in sin, 1. He blamed his wife- "the woman you gave me…" 2. He blamed God: "….the woman you gave me…" 3. As a result of Adam blaming her, she followed his example and blamed the devil when she said to God, "The serpent deceived me and I ate." This spiritual leadership is central to the Christian vision of marriage and family life, a man's spiritual leadership is not a matter of dictatorial power, but of firm and credible spiritual leadership and influence.

The Head (Foundation), The Man, The Husband

A man must be ready to lead his wife and his children in a way that will honor God, demonstrate godliness, inculcate Christian character, and lead his family to desire Christ and to seek God's glory. Spiritual maturity is a mark of true Christian manhood, and a spiritual immature man is, in at least this crucial sense, spiritually just a boy. Personal maturity sufficient to be responsible husbands and father true masculinity is not a matter of exhibiting supposedly masculine characteristics devoid of the context of responsibility. In the Bible, a man is called to fulfill his role as husband and father, unless granted the gift of celibacy for gospel service, the Christian boy is aim for marriage and fatherhood. This is assuredly a counter-cultural assertion, but the role of husband and father is central to manhood. Marriage is unparalleled in its effect on men, as it channels their energies and directs their responsibilities to the devoted covenant of marriage and the grace-filled civilization of the family. They must aspire to be the kind of man a Christian woman would gladly marry and Christian will trust, respect and obey. A real man knows how to earn, manage and respect money, a Christian man understands the danger that comes from the love of money and fulfills his responsibility as a Christian steward. Of course, men come in many sizes and demonstrate different levels of physical strength, but common to all men is a maturity, through which a man demonstrates his masculinity by movement, confidence and strength. A man must be ready to put his physical strength on line to protect his wife and children and to fulfill his God-assigned tasks, a boy must be taught to channel his developing strength and emerging size into a self-consciousness of responsibility, recognizing that that adult strength is to be combined with adult responsibility and true maturity. Sexual maturity sufficient to marry and fulfill God's purposes even as the society celebrates sex in every form and at every age, the true Christian man practices sexual integrity, avoiding pornography, fornication, all forms of sexual promiscuity and corruption. He understands the danger of lust, but rejoices in the sexual capacity and reproductive power God has put within him, committing himself to find a wife, and earn her love, trust and admiration — and eventually to win her hand in marriage. It's critical that men respect this incredible gift, and to protect this gift until, within the context of the holy marriage, they are able to fulfill this gift, love their wives and look to God's gift of children.

Male sexuality separated from the context and integrity of marriage is an explosive and dangerous reality. Ethical maturity sufficient to make responsible decisions, to be a man is to make decisions; one of the fundamental tasks of leadership is decision-making. The indecisiveness of so many contemporary males is evidence of a stunted manhood. Of course, a man does not rush to a decision without thought, consideration or care, but a man does put himself on the line in making a decision — and making it stick. This requires an extension of moral responsibility into mature ethical decision-making that brings glory to God, is faithful to God's Word and is open to moral scrutiny. A real man knows how to make a decision and live with its consequences — even if that means that he must later acknowledge that he has learned by making a bad decision, and then by making the appropriate correction. Worldview maturity sufficient to understand what is really important. An inversion of values marks our postmodern age, and the predicament of modern manhood is made all the more perplexing by the fact that many men lack the capacity of consistent national and International thinking. For the Christian, this is doubly tragic, for our Christian discipleship must be demonstrated in the development of Biblical principle. The Kingdom of GOD, man must understand how to interpret and evaluate issues across the board of politics, economics, morality, entertainment, education and a seemingly endless list of other entities. A man seeks to demonstrate emotional strength, consistency and steadfastness; he must be able to relate to his wife, his children, his peers, his colleagues and a host of others in a way that demonstrates respect, understanding and appropriate love for his family. This will not be learned by entering into the secret world experienced by many male adolescents. Maturity sufficient, to make a contribution to society while the home is an essential and inescapable focus of a man's responsibility, he is also called out of the home into the workplace and the larger world as a witness, and as one who will make a contribution to the common good. God has created human beings as social creatures, and even though our ultimate citizenship is in the Kingdom of Heaven, we must also fulfill our citizenship on earth. Character maturity is sufficient to demonstrate courage under fire. The literature of manhood is replete with stories of courage, bravery and audacity. At least, that's the way it used to be. Now, with manhood both minimalized and marginalized by cultural elite, ideological subversion and media confusion,

The Head (Foundation), The Man, The Husband

we must recapture a commitment to courage that is translated into the real-life challenges faced by the Christian man. At times, this quality of courage is demonstrated when a man risks his own life in defense of others, especially his wife and children, but also anyone who is in need of rescue. More often, this courage is demonstrated in taking a stand under hostile fire, refusing to succumb to the temptation of silence and standing as a model and example to others, who will then be encouraged to stand their own ground. In these days, biblical manhood requires great courage. The prevailing ideologies and worldviews of this age are inherently hostile to Christian truth and are corrosive to Christian faithfulness. It takes great courage for a man to devote himself unreservedly to his wife. It takes great courage to say no to what this culture insists is the rightful pleasures and delights of the flesh. It takes courage to serve as a godly husband and father, to raise children in the nurture and admonition of the Lord. It takes courage to maintain personal integrity in a world that devalues the truth, disparages God's Word, and promises self-fulfillment and happiness only through the assertion of undiluted personal autonomy. A man's true confidence is rooted in the wells of courage, and courage is evidence of character. In the end, a man's character is revealed in the crucible of everyday challenges. For most men, life will also bring moments when extraordinary courage will be required, if he is to remain faithful and true. Biblical maturity sufficient to lead at some level in the church, takes a close look at many churches will reveal that a central problem is the lack of biblical maturity among the men of the congregation and a lack of biblical knowledge that leaves men ill equipped and completely unprepared to exercise spiritual leadership. While God has appointed specific officers for his church — men who are specially gifted and publicly called — every man should fulfill some leadership responsibility within the life of the congregation. For some men, this may mean a less public role of leadership than is the case with others. In any event, a man should be able to teach someone, and to lead in some ministry, translating his personal discipleship into the fulfillment of a godly call. There is a role of leadership for every man in every church, whether that role is public or private, large or small, official or unofficial. A man should know how to pray before others, to present the Gospel and to stand in the gap where a leadership need is apparent.

The position of the husband in the home and his related responsibilities are quite clearly defined in principle in Ephesians 5:22, 28-31. "Wives submit yourselves to your own husbands, as to the Lord. For the husband is head of the wife, even as Christ is head of the church; and he is the savior of the body. Therefore as the church is subject to Christ, so let wives be to their own husbands in everything. Husbands love your wife as Christ also loved the church and gave himself for it . . . So ought men to love their wives as their own bodies. He who loves his wife loves himself. For no man ever yet hated his own flesh but nourishes and cherishes it, even as the Lord the church . . . For this cause shall a man leave his father and mother and shall be joined unto his wife, and they two shall be one flesh". It is impossible to completely deal with the responsibilities of the husband in a book alone. Let us start with some scriptures that deal with the husband as head of the house. Genesis 3:16, says in part "her desire shall be to man". Then Eph. 5:23, "husband is head of the wife"; then I Tim. 2:11-12, "She shall have no dominion over a man," the only responsibility of the husband is to be HEAD of the house. The head does not mean master as in a master-slave relationship, nor does it mean a relationship like a general to a private in the army and the Head does not mean standing on top of the home. It is a partnership where one is the leader, guide, and director. Not to make that a husband should make any decisions WITHOUT consulting or considering his wife and her wishes. The Husband is the FOUNDATION of the home, which means he takes on all the above responsibilities. The meaning of foundation is to hold up the structure of the home and everything in it. The husband is to love his wife above all other human beings. Consider Eph. 5:25 and 28; and Col. 3:19. These passages teach that the husband is to be considerate and tender. The verses in Ephesians 5 teach that the husband is to cherish his wife. This means that she is to be treated with tenderness and affection. This would mean that since love must be fed, there is to be a warm demonstrative love relationship. The husband has the responsibility of not only demonstrating his love and concern, but telling her. He should not sit in such self-absorption that he does not talk with her and communicate with her socially, mentally, verbally and physically. The husband will demonstrate his love for his wife in other ways, rather than just at the time of sexual relationship.

The Head (Foundation), The Man, The Husband

If this is the only time that affection and consideration is shown, then a wife will get the idea that all a husband is interested in is her body and that she is merely a sex toy. I Peter 3:7, teaches that the husband is to honor his wife. She gave up her name to take yours. Honor means that you should show her respect and this involves courtesy, consideration and emotional support. Be sure that as her husband that you do not hold her up to ridicule in public by the cutting remarks that you make. She wears YOUR name and is to be viewed as part of your body. She is not perfect and you are aware of this. Do not expect perfection, but as Ephesians 4:32 teaches, "Forbear one another". This means to be gentle toward her, control of temper, abstaining from physical violence and restraining a sharp tongue that makes one feel so inferior - are ways by which you can exhibit forbearance. Paul presents another responsibility of husbands in I Timothy 5:8 - "But if any provide not for his own, especially for those of his own household, he has denied the faith and is worse than an infidel". Marriage is a financial venture and the husband has a responsibility to finance or support or provide for his family. This is talking about money. As a husband, your earnings are not your own but belong to your wife as well and your children. The husband is to be active in the area of the discipline and rearing of the children. When the Apostle Paul was giving the qualifications for elders and deacons, he included this statement that is certainly applicable to all men: I Timothy 3:3-5, and he speaks of ruling your own house. Now this discipline should be with love. Many times discipline is administered without love. The Book says in Ephesians 6:4, "Fathers provoke not your children to wrath", and again in Colossians 3:21, "Fathers provoke not your children to anger lest they be discouraged". The husband therefore does not leave all the discipline up to his wife, but shares in the molding and direction of your children. It is not a proper direction of responsibility to say that as the husband I will provide the living and the wife is to take care of the house and children. The husband has duties even after his work is done by which lies in is earning a living to support his family. In fact these duties are a part of his days work. The Kingdom citizen, father should set an example for his family as he earns a living, directs the household with concern for each member, and as he fulfills his role as foundation of the house.

He should see to their spiritual development by the life he lives and the direction in which he leads his family. Your wife is a part of your body - you are a part of each other. For this reason Paul said, "Love your wife". He didn't say if you want to. As you love her, you love yourself and are fulfilling the role that the Lord wanted you to have. In the early hours of man's existence, God said, "It is not good that the man should be alone. I will make for him a suitable helpmeet for him" Genesis 2:18. The beautiful garden would not have been a paradise without Eve. What a lonely existence man would have had without woman. Man has need for companionship, affection, empathy, procreation. It is not good that man should be alone. Naturally, this applies to woman, too. Home is one of the sweetest and fondest words enshrined in human affections. Woman's greatest joy can come in making a happy home for her husband and children. It is very difficult to overestimate the worth of a good woman. Solomon recognized the virtues of a good woman and man's inability to get along without them. He said, "Who can find a virtuous woman? For her price is far above rubies, the heart of her husband does safely trust in her. She will do him good, and not evil, all the days of her life. Her husband is known in the gates, when he sits among the elders of the land" Proverbs 31:10-31. In Proverbs we find such statements as "he who finds a wife, finds a good thing and obtain favor of the Lord" Proverbs 18:22. And "house and riches are the inheritance of fathers, and a prudent wife is from the Lord" Proverbs 19:14. We should not cease in the giving of thanks to the Lord if we have found a prudent wife. How fortunate we are if we have mutual love and companionship in our homes. If we do not have such a home, may God help us to achieve one. The Bible says love is as strong as death. Jealousy is cruel as the grave. Many waters cannot quench love; neither can the floods drown it. (Solomon 8:6-7). Solomon also said live joyfully with your wife, whom you love, all the days of the life of your vanity (Ecclesiastes 9:9). If the home is not a happy place, someone has failed. Peter gave us instructions on how to live together harmoniously. He said, "Husbands, dwell with them (your wives) according to knowledge, giving honor to the wife as to the weaker vessel and as being heirs together of the grace of life, that your prayers be not hindered" II Peter 3:7. She is not weaker in character and intellect, but she is weaker physically and man must understand her needs and limitations. He must also be aware of her ability to help him.

The Head (Foundation), The Man, The Husband

He must also use his abilities in helping her. Wise men show an interest when their wives speak up, and weigh their wisdom, for many times their wisdom out-weighs that of their mates. Sometimes we rob ourselves of the happiness GOD the Father intended for us because we have not learned to enjoy the companionship of our Godly mates. Pitiful is the man or woman who exploits his mate and reveals secrets that should be kept between them. It is unbecoming and certainly not Christ minded to downgrade the opposite sex in storytelling and off-color jokes. We are God's creation, each with a specific assignment. We're not in competition, and the God fearing woman is not seeking a false liberation, but is happy and fulfilled in the role that God gave her. Many of our frustrations are mental as well as physical ills, brought upon us by a lack of "love and companionship" in the home. Our greatest joy should come to us through our working together as husband and wife, and praying together with common interests and common goals. God has given us laws for our well-being, for God knows greater than we do, for the word of GOD tells us best "For My thoughts are not your thoughts, nor are your ways My ways, declares the Lord. "For as the heavens are higher than the earth so are my ways higher than your ways and My thoughts than your thoughts. God knows the things that are good for us and the things that make us happy (Matthew 6:8; Ephesians 5:25). Husband, are you treating your wife as an equal and granting her your highest honor? If not God says he will not answer your prayers! (1Pet.3:7), Selfishness is a marriage killer. For many men they think they are better than their wives simply because they are men. These men have made a serious judgment error. Husbands must tell their wives how important and valuable she is to you. Watch for the loving smile on her face when you do! Solomon said, "An excellent wife, who can find? For her worth is far above jewels. The heart of her husband trusts in her, and he will have no lack of gain." Prov. 31:10-11 Notice how the wise husband trusts his wife's judgments and realize how fortunate he is to have her.

Dysfunctional Headship

The World Says

Gives orders without asking or permitting questions

Makes demands

Dishes out directives

Lays down the law, cracks

Pushes and manipulates

You do, you must do", or "Yours is not to wonder why, yours is but to do or die"

Proper Headship

God's Way

Asks questions

 Seeks to truly hear

 Suggests alternatives

 Desires input-learns from others

Delegate authority &responsibility;

Respects freedom & dignity of others,

Keep reigns on loose tongues

Secure self-identity

Understand his authority

View challenges as positive

Value willing cooperation

Works for open agreement and understanding

Lead, attract, and persuade personal relationships in side-by-side identification

Say, "Come, let's do, we might have done, can we try"

Depend on internal integrity to motivate others

Generate acceptance, co-operation, and reconciliation

Unite and help people relate to each other

Lead by example, understanding and kindness

Ask others to do only those things he has already done (like Jesus)

Your highest allegiance, beneath GOD, must be to your wife, not your family and friends. (Gen 2:24).You must consistently tell your wife how important & valuable she is to you. (Phil 2:3; Prov. 31:10-11)

God gave women the authority to make important decisions too:

They are workers in and managers of the home:

1 Ti 5:14: (Greek: oijkodespotevw "to rule/manage the house")

Tit 2:5 (Greek: oikodespotes literally, "house ruler")

A wife's judgment can be better than her husband's: Nabal & Abigail: 1 Sam 25:3,17,25,32

The Head (Foundation), The Man, The Husband

You should hold your wife's love by the same means that you won it. (Song. of Sol. 5:10-16). Men pursue their future bride with ceaseless attention once married the husband views marriage as a goal accomplished an on to other of life's challenges. He then gives his ceaseless attention to the job, the boys or anything but his wife. She on the other hand viewed marriage not as a goal met, but as the beginning of a relationship. She viewed his ceaseless attention as a down payment of attentions to come. He viewed it as a means to merely get her to say "I DO". The man really WON the love of his future wife. He looked good because he groomed his appearance for her. He smelled good, because he regularly bathed and gargled, and he spoke words of "sweetness" to his love. But give many husbands a few years of marriage and they let their appearance and hygiene slip. But worst of all the sweetness towards their wife is gone. The wife speaks out to her friends, "Things changed after we said 'I do'!" You must warm up your wife in the day with words of kindness. Buy your wife flowers on a regular basis. You should at all times establish family discipline with your wife's help. (2 Timothy 3:15; Ephesians 6:4; Deuteronomy 6:6-9) Few would argue that the wife is the primary parent involved in the daily task of interacting with the children. But God has placed the father as the head of the household and foundation of the home, and that means that you must work hard alongside of your wife in establishing family discipline, that is you the instructor and the wife the teacher. Many fathers leave the majority of the work of raising the kids up to the wife. In child custody cases, the mother almost always get control of the kids, not because she is a better parent, but because she is the one who has been most involved with them. God commands fathers in Ephesians 6:4 "And, fathers, do not provoke your children to anger; but bring them up in the discipline and instruction of the Lord." You must be directly involved with your children. And then be careful not to "provoke" them to anger, because you have not really taken the time to understand exactly what happened and why. Some fathers alienate their children because they hastily dish out too harsh a punishment because they want to get back to their TV show or reading the paper. To these husbands, children are an interruption imposed upon him by the wife. You are the Foundation of the Home! Train up a child in the way he should go, even when he is old he will not depart from it. Prov. 22:6.

"PLEASE, DADDY, WON'T YOU GO?"

A little girl's bright shining eyes with face aglow,
Says: "Daddy, It's time for church-Let's Go!
They teach us there of Jesus' love, of how he died for all,
Upon the cruel cross to save those who on Him will call."
"Oh, no," said Daddy, "Not today. I've worked hard all week,
And I must have one day of rest; and I'm going to the creek.
For there I can relax and rest; and fishing is fine they say.
So run along; don't bother me, we'll go to church someday."
Well months and years have passed away,
But Daddy hears that plea no more;
"Let's go to Bible school." Those childhood days are over.
And Daddy's grown old, life's almost through,
He finds time to go to church, but what does daughter do?
She says: "Oh Daddy, not today-I stayed up half the night;
I know you know that church can wait...you understand my plight!
Then Daddy lifts a trembling hand to brush away the tears,
As again he hears the pleading voice, distinctly through the years.
He sees a small girl's shining face upturned, with eyes aglow,
As she says, "It's time for Bible school; please,
Daddy, won't you go?"

You are the "FOUNDATION OF THE HOME" men you must exercise the express power of GOD working through you and me. The skills and abilities we were created with, to manage the worlds. To take on that attitude is to take on the Citizen of the Kingdom of GOD.

CHAPTER II
The Helpmeet, The Woman And The Wife

As God set the stage for man, He then gave man a suitable helper first and not a wife, in fact it was God who gave man the suitable helper but then He gave it over to Adam to name her and it was Adam who called the suitable helper, woman and wife as noted in Gen. 2:15-25...read it carefully. So as the woman comes on the scene she was not made like the man, from the dust of the ground and the breath of life blown in her nostrils, the bible says she was fashioned (Gen. 2:22), the Hebrew word for fashioned is "Yatsar" which means to frame, form or fashion. Now to fashion means to take special care and attention to form and this is what God did in putting the woman together not from the dust but from Adam himself performing the first open surgery recorded on earth. As she was completely fashioned God gave the woman over to man because He made covenant that man was not created to be alone so therefore He created a suitable helper for the sole purpose to help man maintain his position on earth. This is the primary aspect for the woman to be a suitable helper to the man, this is not to say the woman can't obtain skills and abilities in the world "NO", this means in all that the woman does no matter how great in skills she achieve in the world, in the Kingdom of God she is created to be a suitable helper to a man, more so your husband. Many women fall very short in this area because of not studying Gods word properly to know the wisdom of things, which is the application of all things in your life, which also bring you maturity in God's word.

God took special time to place in the women every component needed to sustain her threefold position as a suitable helper, a women and a wife, in these positions holds the keys of success in a man's life to maintain his position as the man God purposed the man to be here on earth. This is why it is very important to note that the man and the woman must at all times line up with Kingdom of Heaven first to stay intact with the culture of Heaven for the purpose of exercising the Kingdom of God within us.

SUITABLE HELPMEET, The first of the position, the suitable helper is the most important of the three, it is in this position that wisdom of GOD is found to conduct righteousness, maturity in the woman to become the proper wife, a virtuous woman. A suitable helper exercises calm, compassion, submission the man needs to live in the world given to him to dominate. The suitable helper search and research all things out in the assignment given to her by her head or provider, the suitable helper studies and meditate properly to know and understand this position as she is established under the guide lines of the "Kingdom of GOD." A suitable helper upon operating under the Kingdom of God guide lines take pride in submission to her husband because she knows her positions. In this life God has ordain pain and difficulty, when man and woman come together in marriage this union is not for the sole purpose to love one another until death, in fact when Christ gave himself over to the world for sacrifice of sin to die on the cross with sole purpose was to freeing man from the bondage of devils control, the first thing Christ did in the beginning of His Ministry was to be baptize, soon after Jesus was baptize He went straight into being tempted by devil setting the stage for difficulty in one's life first before peace and love. This is why the bible says in Job 8:7; Your beginnings will seem humble, so prosperous will your future be, what Christ was establishing was how life begins since the fall of Adam, in difficulty so when a man and woman say I do they are saying I do not to peace and love but the transition of a difficult road ahead. The road of pain and suffering in the beginning, that's why God place first the suitable helper before the position of woman and wife because God knew in difficulty help was needed the most, not just having a woman on the scene or just having bragging rights to say you are married and attempting to live happily ever after, to brag about a beautiful woman or an handsome man.

The Helpmeet, The Woman, The Wife

You step into the arena of death and destruction, a world of trouble Paul says about marriage "It is trouble he says", so it is important for the woman and wife to know in the life you have here on this earth, you were created as a suitable helper by God and Adam is who called you, woman and wife not GOD. In difficulty you are to expect the best but prepare for the worst, in difficulty you are to prepare for war and there will be the wounded and as a suitable helper you must know your family (husband & child), know every aspect of your household, its need and wants. Know what's good and what's not good, be very attentive to the complete wellbeing of the members of your family, know what to do for your family, understand why you are doing these things and above how to do all for your family. Be short of nothing in skills and abilities in taking care of your family, that in doing so your kids can see and do righteously. Your home should not be a place of busy body people traveling in and out as though you are in a grocery store, your home is the original place of worship and just has you travel quietly and respectfully through the secondary building we call the church house, we must sustain our home just as great. This is why God declared a suitable helper and not just a helper, a suitable helper means the woman is proper for that particular man, not any man that comes along, that one man God assigns you, who is suitable or proper. The problem many face in carrying out this position is first devil, sifting many like wheat and so many go through this ordain difficulty and are told, just as Christ said to Peter. "when you come out strengthened your brothers," in other words what Christ was saying when you get through this battle you will be well battle ready for more so get your family prepared for the next round, cause "It AIN'T OVER." devil don't stop seeking God for permission to attack, he knows his destination, which is the Lake of Fire, he's just not try to go by himself so he seeks company. Man has a twenty-four hour time table he must operate upon every day of his life. This time is as follows, 1). Eight hours to Work (to the Head/Foundation)......2). Eight hours of Service between Man and GOD (to the Man) .....3). Eight hours of Rest (to the Husband). For the threefold position of the female, to line up with the threefold position of the male is as follows 1). Eight hours of Work, is to the Head and Helpmeet.....2). Eight hours of Service between Man and God, is to the Man and the Woman.......3). Eight hours of Rest, is to the Husband and the Wife.

The role of the Helpmeet is helping man maintain his position on earth as the manager of GODS business in the world, in other words manage the earth. As GOD laid out the purpose and plan with Adam was to manage the earth, GOD then said "It is not good for the man to be alone; I will make a suitable helper for him. Gen. 2:18. It is clear that in management of the great earth as great as we men are in our positions GOD has given us, it was fitting that we receive help better known as the "Helpmeet." The Helpmeet is uniquely knowledgeable to service, why because GOD instilled this skill within her, given her the quality skill set of knowing how to handle WORK. In every aspect of what she does, it is done in the capacity of helping; she can be CEO, Manager of any position held it will always result to helping to achieve the goal. Once given a platform the Helpmeet can quickly spring into action and began toward progress. It is vitally important that she has a platform from the Headship of man in order to perform her skills properly. Note even in the worst conditions she is able to adjust to assist the cause. Once given the right platform that would best suit her skills, and would sustain humbleness in her that would enhance the Headship of the man to maintain his life before GOD, as he was created to do. The Helpmeets purpose is to measure the skills of the man, measuring his strengths and his weakness and build on them. The Helpmeet has been created with skills of enhancement that is naturally in her to help the man establish his Headship. During the "Eight hour of Work" in man's 24 hour service time frame of his everyday life, this means finance, home building, and business establishment. This is business management, which is a very important part of GOD's purpose and plan. Luke. 6:48. Finances is the number one root cause of today's family break-ups, which leads to home and business loss. "He who troubles his own house will inherit wind, and the foolish will be servant to the wise hearted." Prov. 11:29. Every man needs a suitable helper but not just need a helper, but a help meet that perfectly fits. The helpmeet is supposed to suit the Headship of the man and not prison him. Many women like to seize authority from the husband and take charge of his life and leadership of the home. Every domineering attitude and character will be a destroyer of the family and enables the helpmeet improper role in the man's life. She is supposed to complement the man and not compound his life. God saw the man needed help, sending the helpmeet forth to help the Headship of man. By implication, the helpmeet is to fill the vacuum in the Headship of man's life.

The Helpmeet, The Woman, The Wife

She is to help the man in the areas of weakness. But many women instead of complimenting have become problems themselves, thereby, compounding the man's life. Every helpmeet is to be a problem solver to the Headship of the man, burden bearer not a burden the carrier. The suitable helper is supposed to make the Headship of man's life sweeter and not bitter. She is in his life to add spices to it. Therefore, every helpmeet should do what is necessary to make the Headship of the man life sweet and not bitter. The suitable helper is supposed to help the Headship of the man, to fulfill his dream and not destroy it. The suitable helper is supposed to help the Headship of the man maintain focus and not to lose focus by distractions. There is always the tendency to be distracted from one's vision in life. The suitable helper is a tension reliever and not a tension builder. The suitable helper is supposed to be a psychiatrist and counselor to the Headship of the man. The help meet is designed to be supportive and not subtractive. The suitable helper is a keeper of home and not a trouble maker. The suitable helper is to tidy up things and not make them untidy. A suitable helper should adapt to the Headship man's life and vision. A suitable helper should be good company to the Headship of man. The suitable helper is not to compete with the Headship of man. The suitable helper joins forces with the Headship of man to procreate. The suitable helper is a builder and not a destroyer. **THE WOMAN.**, When the wounded family comes in, the position of the woman steps in with her nurturing ways and means, the woman releases the love, the care, the compassion for the need of the family doing this time of difficulty, she express peace and joy to the kids who so yearn for her attention 24hrs a day. She carries the burden of comfort to every corner of the home that where ever devil seeks to enter he will know that there is a battle ready suitable helper, woman and wife in that place with a love for her family and that she will not be compromised. The woman is the engineer of the home, as the Bibles says— in Prov. 14:1, "The wise woman builds her house, but with her own hands the foolish one tears hers down," But Prov. 9:1-6 says— " Wisdom has built her house; she has set up its seven pillars. She has prepared her meat and mixed her wine; she has also set her table. She has sent out her servants, and she calls from the highest point of the city, "Let all who are simple come to my house!"

To those who have no sense she says," come; eat my food and drink of the wine I have mixed. Forsake your folly and live, and proceed in the way of understanding." The woman given the proper supplies from her husband sets the standards as to how the house runs or operates amongst the children, the husband sets the instructions out to the suitable helper which in intern dissect the instruction to the simplest form to the woman who then gathers all information transitioning it in her thinking, to her attitude, to her philosophy, to behavior and her action. This gives the woman what she needs to build her house in to a home, fulfilling all needs to the every aspect of the "Husband and Child" so that her virtuous ways and means can exceed to the ways of the Old as Paul says. In— 1 Pet 3:1-6; GODLY LIVING in the same way, you wives, be submissive to your own husbands so that even if any of them are disobedient to the word, they may be won without a word by the behavior of their wives, as they observe your chaste and respectful behavior. Your adornment must not be merely external-braiding the hair, and wearing gold jewelry, or putting on dresses; but let it be the hidden person of the heart, with the imperishable quality of a gentle and quiet spirit, which is precious in the sight of God. For in this way in former times the holy woman also, who hoped in God, used to adorn themselves, being submissive to their own husbands; just as Sarah obeyed Abraham, calling him lord, and you have become her children if you do what is right without being frightened by any fear. What 1 Peter 3 is saying here is that this is the intended way of life for the woman to operate in; it is this mannerism that is acceptable with God and pleasing in his sight. Such differences or division hinders the prayers that the family seeks God to interfere in the families affairs; the woman is the heart of this threefold position of the female (suitable helper, woman and wife). But it is vitally important for the woman in her position to operate to the fullest, it is important to understand the husband's instructions for such instructions come from God as the husband is in line with the kingdom of God. The woman in her early rise is for the sake of instructions for the days family business, everything about the woman in her position is to transcend the family as to God the Father, in the name of Christ Jesus under the instructions of the Holy Spirit which is the instructions to the husbands which is instructions to the suitable helper, woman and wife to maintain the family. The greatest downfall of the family is division; division is to set apart; to separate, this is what we witness in the Garden of Eden with Adam and Eve.

The Helpmeet, The Woman, The Wife

This division was so catastrophic to the human race, not God's purpose and plan but to man, leaving Adam and Eve under a great punishment that still stands today Gen. 3:1-23; (this is not a part of the curse) which redirected God original intention for the foundation of the family, altering temporarily, how the family should function. This fall occurred by way of the two standing together as one to eat of the fruit that made them like the trinity, as God said knowing good and evil. This fall came by way of the suitable helper not the woman or the wife, "The wise woman builds her house, but with her own hands the foolish one tears hers down" (Prov. 14:1). Some of the world finest couples are divorced more than once and their families have been sacrificed for their job. This is hard enough for a man, but a woman has the authority of her husband and the authority she serves at work. Some would say that they have no problem in this area, but the rise in broken homes says much different. God intended the home to be the center of a women's world. This has been greatly attacked even in the days of the New Testament. In Titus 5:14 younger women were encouraged to marry, bear children, and guide the home so that they would not be attacked by the enemy. In Titus 2:5, older women were to encourage the younger women to love their husband and children and to be keepers of the home that the word of God might not be blasphemed. Why? Because they were not doing what Paul was trying to do, lead them back to God's design. It is when we as a society have rejected His plan that our plan will be in the opposite direction and will lead to disaster. One of these ways is when we justify women working outside of the home. 40 years ago most young women were graduating from high school, getting married and starting to raise a family. Today, however, our society is teaching them that they need a career to fall back on just in case their marriage does not last. What does the word of God say will happen when women work outside the home? The woman does not meet her highest potential; God designed the woman to be a helpmeet for her husband. Often you hear women say that they are tired of being identified as somebody's wife, and they have forgotten that they will be the only one in the world that will hold that title in the family? If a husband were to lose their job, the company would just hire another person to replace him and within a short time he would be forgotten. If the family loses the husband, they would be damaged and would never be their best in moving forward.

The absence would be felt for years to come. The women of the house would then form an independent spirit; the scriptures tell us that for Husband to love your wives. . . . Wives submit to your husband (Col. 3:18-19). Not even men are to be independent. Nowhere in scripture does God want an independent person, but our adversary, the devil, promotes independence from God. This is a damaging philosophy in marriages today. When a woman does not think she needs her husband or children, she will lose her love for them. This is one of the reasons why a growing number of couples do not have children. It reduces their independence and increases their so called freedom. She becomes financially unwise; this leads to a wakeup call to men that they should not leave their wives, because of the hardships that they will bring upon them. Remember, she is your companion (best friend) and the wife of your covenant (Mal. 2:14). Many people lose sight on understanding how family should survive any level income, and or learn how to actually do better than most with two incomes. The Women's greatest asset is hindered, with time is our most valuable asset and the Bible tells us to number our days that we may apply our hearts to wisdom (Psalms 90:12). God has placed in every women the gifts and talents to teach and train her children, not the daycare system. Scripture teaches that when a child is left to himself, he will bring his mother to shame (Proverbs 29:15). The Hebrew word for left is translated Shalach which means to send away. When women send their children out from their God given responsibilities it will bring shame to her. Women cannot fulfill their responsibility unless their husbands establish a platform for them to do that. We, as a nation, have forgotten the influencing power women have over her children and what mighty things she can accomplish for her community and the Kingdom of God when she has a platform in the home. Women can be tempted to transfer her affections away from their husbands. This is something that happens all over our nation: women having affairs with men in the work place. This is a major cause that lead up to an affair. As people work together, they talk and become friends. As problems develop at home, usually financial, discussions take place and soon she starts comparing the men at work to her husband. Even though an affair may never take place, she has misplaced some of her affections away from her husband and has damaged her marriage. Soon the husband realizes that she doesn't depend on him like she used to. Distrust and even jealousy raises its ugly head.

The Helpmeet, The Woman, The Wife

When women get together and talk about their husband's it's usually in a negative outcome. They disgrace themselves, because they are degrading the one that they vowed to love, cherish and honor for the rest of their lives before GOD. This brings on an automatic punishment by way of adultery from the hand of GOD. When Adam and Eve sinned, God cursed man that he would work by the sweat of his brow and the woman would have pain in child bearing. Now the working woman has taken both of the curses upon herself. God's word never said that women could not perform an outside job or that they weren't as smart as men. In fact, God has put women in roles that were designed for men when they would not lead. This book is for men and women who are committed to Jesus Christ and are seeking to make a difference in their lives for Him. Jesus said seek first the Kingdom of heaven and his righteousness and all these things shall be added to you Matt. 6:33. We as Christians need to stop following after the things of the world and start to deny ourselves pick up the Cross and follow Christ. If you find this offensive, then this message is not for you. When we began to put our lives under Biblical principles, only then can God step in and bless you and your family. Simply because of you showing honor and glory to which He is, GOD Almighty. We can truly be the light of the world that He wants us to be. When children see that parents are committed to each other and they can come home to a mother who is there to make them the best that they can be, then they will rise up and call her blessed. To the separated or divorced women, this message is for your husband's to return to their vows and allow God to be the God of love that He longs to be. To the widow, this message is for family, friends and the Church to return to their Citizen of the Kingdom of GOD duties and support these women. **"THE WIFE,"** the wife plays a ventricle part to the husband only; she is in complete harmony with the husband that they display a unity in line with the trinity. This unity holds to no separation, no division, no departure unless by way of death or adultery or adulteress according to 1 Cor. 7 chapter, just as God the Father, God the Son, and God the Holy Spirit hold in unity this is the same criteria God holds over the "Husband" and the "Wife." The wife is strictly designated to the husband, her position is to see the total need of the husband as 1 Cor. 7: 2-6— "But because of immoralities, each man is to have his own wife, and each woman is to have her own husband.

The Kingdom Culture Community

The husband must fulfill his duty to his wife, and likewise also the wife to her own husband. The wife does not have authority over her own body, but the husband does; and likewise also the husband does not have authority over his own body, but the wife does. Stop depriving one another, except by agreement for a time, so that you may devote yourselves to prayer, and come together again so that Satan will not tempt you because of your lack of self-control. (1Cor.7:5-6). It is vitally important in this position of the wife to stay focus to her husband, just as it is stated in the punishment Christ set upon Adam and Eve upon the fall, Gen. 3:16-19 To the woman (wife) He said, "I will greatly multiply your pain in childbirth, In pain you will bring forth children; Yet your desire will be for your husband, and he will rule over you." Then to Adam He said, "Because you have listened to the voice of your wife, and have eaten from the tree about which I command you, saying, "you shall not eat from it; Cursed is the ground because of you; In toil you will eat of it all the days of your life. Both thorns and thistles it shall grow for you; And you will eat the plants of the field; by the sweat of your face you will eat bread, till you return to the ground, because from it you were taken; for you are dust, and to dust you shall return." When a wife is declared a wife this is the first phase of difficulty she and her husband must transition through. It is nowhere in bible that says this punishment is removed because it was Christ who set the punishment upon man and woman because of the fall and if you believe it to be removed then check and see if the woman is no longer experiencing pain during the birthing process, see if by not her eyes being for her husband only no longer brings conflict and check to see if the husband no longer rule as he is in his proper place (not out of place). Check the husband to see if he no longer sweat when working hard for his family and check the grave to see if the body is no longer dust as it returns to the ground. When you discover it all still stands then you can begin as a husband or a wife to refocus your attention to the first phase of marriage, "The Pain of Difficulty." Too many times we as men and woman blame others for our downfalls just as Adam said to Christ in the Garden, "It was the woman that you gave me he said," we are not doing enough of self-improvement, self-evaluation. We spend too much time focusing on the outside of our homes and not enough time on the inside. In other words the problem is not with others the problem is with us, the one who you look at in the mirror.

The Helpmeet, The Woman, The Wife

Despite all things you must first make sure you are spotless and blameless before blame, the wife for instance operates in many of her ways by way of emotion, and she is an emotional being, many times in difficulty her reaction is based on how she feels. The problem with that kind of reaction is that feelings don't think they just "REACT," while the men operate upon our thinking process, what's in our head or mind. The only time a man operates off of emotions is when he is dealing with a woman; this brings major pain and difficulty in most marriages and brings them to an end, the lack of wisdom, knowledge and understanding to the operation of each other's ways and means. In the Bible it is clear that God created man and woman to face difficulty, God has ordained for you and for me struggle. We cannot run away from difficulty in this life, drugs, alcohol, excessive sex, pleasure seeking is a means of running from reality, from your responsibilities to face difficulty. Whenever we face a difficulty and overcome that difficulty we improve our character and we improve ourselves. The key word is to face the difficulty, when you face something you look at it, when you face something you summon the strength of your spiritual being, you will, to absolutely face and overcome that stumbling block that is in the way of your progress. The question is how do you face your difficulty as a husband or a wife, it does not matter how young or how old you are if you been on this earth a while you got difficulty. See! you don't have to be here a long time to have difficulty, you can be a young person and have difficulty, how do you face these marital matters, if you turn your back on your difficulty, then what benefit is that too you?...what affect does this have upon your husband or wife? Anytime we turn away from overcoming our difficulties we deteriorate our character and our will, because it is the will in man that is the connection to the Lord of creation. Man and woman are the only ones in existence that God gives the power to will and if you don't face the difficulty, you deteriorate your will and if you deteriorate your will, you deteriorate the power within yourselves and if you deteriorate the power within yourselves then you become nothing, you become lower than the animal because they function from instinct in accord with the nature in which they were created, but when your will is destroyed you don't become an animal, you become lower than an animal and you are totally out of sync from the nature in which you were created.

The Kingdom Culture Community

Struggle is ordain to us but after any pain and suffering there is always joy in the end with God, nothing last forever. God never gives a difficult time and get you through without given you peace, a time where he gives you some ease. In the life of a chicken, that chicken has got to peck on the egg break the shell to come forward, you and I can break the shell easy but it is a struggle for the life within that shell to peck and peck to break free from within that shell. A bird struggles to come to birth, then it must struggles to fly, the caterpillar struggle to get out the cocoon and human life struggles to get free of the womb. Coming to birth is painful, for every woman who has had a child the birthing process is painful for you the woman, but if the child could talk and if that child could tell you how hard it was on it, it would tell you a very hard story. It's painful for the child to come to birth but the child can't talk about its pain, but it's in pain coming forward. God has ordain pain to attend every stage of progress, no pain...no progress...no pain...no higher elevation...run from pain...you run from progress...run from pain...you run from development...if you face your difficulty which is painful, you can overcome it, there is no human being on earth that doesn't have the capabilities to overcome the difficulty if you summon the power of God within you against that object that stands in the way of your progress and MOVE, there is no one that can keep you from what God has ordain for you…"If you face the difficulty." The first duty of a wife is her husband. Your husband is your assignment. His dream and vision becomes your dream also. You as a wife must understand that you are in your husband's life to help him succeed in the pursuit of his God-given assignment. Your role is a supportive role. You're personal vision must be in line with your husband's vision and not contrary. Contrary vision will bring conflicts. The duty of the wife as a suitable helper is to help the husband at such times to focus on his assignment. The wife therefore is not to become a distraction to the husband through her nagging, wrong habits and character. When Jesus was confronted with the question of marriage and divorce he answered by taking them back to the beginning when God created man and woman. "Some Pharisees came to him to test him. They said, is it lawful for a man to divorce his wife for any and every reason? "Haven't you read, he replied, that at the beginning the Creator made them male and female, and said, for this reason a man will leave his father and mother and be united to his wife, and the two will become one flesh? So they are no longer two, but one.

The Helpmeet, The Woman, The Wife

Therefore what God has joined together, let man not separate" (Mt. 19:3-6) for one to understand the success of marriage, one needs to understand the purpose of marriage. To understand God's purpose of marriage, we need to go back to the beginning of the creation of man and the woman. "The Lord God said, 'It is not good for the man to be alone, I will make a helper suitable for him. "(Gen. 2:18) In other words: The ideal wife should fit the husband perfectly, she is supposed to complete the man's life and not complicate it, and the man is not complete without the wife. The wife is to fill the gap in the man's life and take care of the things the man cannot take care of. Wives are supposed to be burden bearers and not a burden to their husband's. Understand your role and play it well. Help your husband's to be what he is called to be. The wife is supposed to help the husband cool off and not put the heat on him. When the husband is under pressure, the wife is supposed to help the husband. Every wife should know how to help her husband at such times, when a man is under pressure; he does not perform well at work nor think clearly. He does not need the pressure from the wife but encouragement. Every husband must be humble enough to receive counsel from his wife. Every man needs somebody to share his feelings, frustration and dreams with. The wife should be able to play her supportive role with her care and counsel. The suitable wife is supposed to satisfy the husband sexually and keep him from spilling his life in the streets. "Drink water from your own cistern, running water from your own well. Should your springs overflow in the streets, your streams of water in the public squares? Let them be yours alone, never to be shared with strangers. May your fountain be blessed and may you rejoice in the wife of your youth. A loving doe, a graceful deer -- may her breast satisfy you always, may you ever be captivated by her love. Lack of sex has led many marriages to collapse. Betting with sex is evil. Giving yourself to your husband only after he has met your need or because you want something from him is very wrong. If you are doing that, you are no different from the street prostitutes, who sell their bodies for money. Your duty is to make your husband happy. Sex is not only for making babies. It is for strengthening the bond of love between husband and wife. The good wife is supposed to be an addition and not a minus. Psalm113:9; Prov. 31:10-31.

The Kingdom Culture Community

Every good wife is supposed to take charge of the house keeping maintenance. It is sad to note that the woman who is supposed to be organizing and keeping the home is the one scattering and disorganizing the home. The wife is to help the husband accomplish his assignment and not to hinder it. Check yourselves wives to be sure you are a suitable helper to your husband. If you are not, then go to work on yourself immediately. Husband, allow your wives to perform their duties in your life and home. It takes God to change people, becoming more like Christ is the pathway to marital bliss. Your children are the blessings and responsibilities of your marriage. Your children's habits and character depends on your investment of love, time and money into their lives. Time and effort invested in making yourselves compatible is a good investment that will definitely pay off in the end. The spirit of your family life in following Christ Jesus will determine how far your marriage will receive God's support. Invest love and time in helping one another overcome weakness. Give room for failure knowing that you too do fail sometimes, and you will always want your spouse to understand and bear with you. Say and do to your spouse what you will have them say and do to you. The Wife's responsibility to the Husband is to submit herself to her own husbands, as to the Lord, Therefore as the church is subject unto Christ, so let the wives be to their own husbands in everything, "nevertheless let everyone of you in particular so love his wife even as himself; and the wife will see that she reverence her husband. Likewise you wives, be in subjection to your own husbands. None of this teaches that women are inferior in intellect, but that her feminine quality supersedes her for being well endowed for leadership. The subjection does not mean servitude; it is not the relationship of master and slave or as a maid or servant. Hers is recognition of the husband's leadership, wisdom and tenderness. He should be as loving toward her as Christ loved the church. At this point, there are several privileges that belong to the wife. For instance, she is to be loved like Christ loved the church as commanded in Ephesians 5:25. She is to be honored as none other in I Peter 3:7 and she is to be praised by her family, Prov. 31:28. In Titus 2:4 we read, "That (the aged women) may teach the young women to be sober, to love their husbands, to love their children, to be discreet, chaste, keepers at home, good, obedient to their own husbands, that the word of God be not blasphemed".

The Helpmeet, The Woman, The Wife

The responsibility of a wife is "To love her husband" this is a command too often equated by men to believe it is only a sexual relationship and in the mind of some women, that is all they think they are good for. To love your husband means that you are a partner with him, working together toward a common goal. Then you can be appreciative of his actions, efforts and work in supporting the family. You will do all that you possibly can do to see that they are comfortable and happy when they come home." Love your children", is a command men think to provide for the family financially, wives stay home and steer the children. This might often be considered a no thank you kind of job. This is an area in which you can excel as well as the man earns the living and supports the family, you take care of the children while he is gone to work and make the house comfortable by keeping it pleasant and enjoyable. Yes, children can become exasperating at times, but remember, they are children who are still developing and learning. They need that sober guiding hand of the mature mother who lets them know that they are the objects of her love and concern. Being obedient to her husband, points out the closeness of the two. This is not indicating that You can't and do not have any thoughts of your own the idea is that as a husband and wife work together and that you are not constantly pulling in an opposite direction. This obedience does not mean that you are a slave or an indentured servant, but rather that you are sharing a mutual goal. The sensitive nature of the word obedient is tempered by the display of love and affection that the husband shows his wife. Being keepers of the home is a command that indicates a divided responsibility. His job seems to be to go out and earn the living and provide for his family while she looks after the home. Even though a wife may or may not work outside of the home in what we call public work, she is still vital to the income of the family. This means she is vitally important to the overall success of the family. When God created woman, she was taken from the rib of man as is described in the book of Genesis. She was not taken from his foot that she could be crushed underneath his heel in bitterness. Neither was she taken from his head so that she might rule over him. She was not taken from the hand, that she might continually fill the position of waiting upon him. She was taken from the rib of man that she might be by his side continually to be loved and is to respond as a part of his body. Husbands and wives are a part of each other inside and outside of the home.

The Kingdom Culture Community

Home is where the great is small and the small is great. Home is where our stomachs get three meals a day and our hearts a thousand. Home is a place where a world of strife is shut out and a world of love shut in. Home is where we complain the most, but has the greatest blessings. Expect your husband to give you as many luxuries as your father have given you after many years of hard labor. (Phil 4:11; Amos 4:1) You should work hard to build your house with the husband that you have, not fantasizing about "the one that could have been". (Prov. 14:1) Remember that the approval of your husband is more to you than the side glances of some strangers. (Ezek 16:32; 2 Pet 2:14). You should not yell at your husband but should be a gentle and quiet spirit. (1 Pet 3:1-4).Let no one or thing say to you that you are having a difficult time addressing things. (1 Pet 5:9). Do not fail to dress up for your husband to please him, as you did before marriage. (Song. of Sol. 4:9-11). Submit to your husband from the heart and allow him to be head of the household. (Col 3:18; 1 Pet 3:6; Eph 5:33). Assure your husband and others that he is the greatest man alive. (Phil 2:3; Song. of Sol. 5:9-16).What due does a man owe his wife?
Tell her how pretty she is
Take her out on romantic dinners
Tell her how much you love her
Tell her how much she means to you
Just think, God in His wisdom thought it best that a man should leave his father and mother and cleave to his wife, that the two should become one flesh, He created a help meet for the man... this is what men must remember today.

CHAPTER III

The Child, The Teen
And
The Adult

The Childhood and youth of Jesus were spent in a little mountain village. There was no place on earth that would not have been honored by His presence. The palace of kings would have been privileged in receiving Christ as a guest. But He passed by the homes of wealth, the courts of royalty, and the renowned seats of learning, to make His home in absence of Nazareth. Wonderful in its significance is the brief record of Christ early life: "The child grew strong in spirit, filled with wisdom: and the grace of God was upon Him." In the sunlight of His Father's countenance, Jesus "increased in wisdom, stature, and in great favor with God." Luke 2:52. His mind was active and penetrating, with a thoughtfulness and wisdom beyond His years. Yet His character was/and is beautiful. The power of mind and body developed gradually, in keeping with the laws of childhood. As a child, Jesus manifested a peculiar disposition. His willing hands were ever ready in serving others. He manifested a patience that nothing could disturb, and a truthfulness that would never sacrifice integrity. In principle firm beyond a rock, His life revealed the grace of unselfish life. With deep earnestly the mother of Jesus watched the revealed nature of His power, and beheld the perfection upon His character. With delight she sought to encourage that bright, receptive mind. Through the Holy Spirit she received wisdom to co-operate with the heavenly agencies in the development of this child, who could claim only God as His Father. From the earliest times the faithful in Israel had given much care to the education of the youth. The Lord had directed that even from babyhood the children should be taught, His goodness and His greatness, especially as revealed in His law, and shown in the history of Israel. Song, prayer and lessons from the Scriptures were to be adapted to opening minds.

Fathers and mothers were to instruct their children that the law of God is an expression of His power and authority, and as they received the principles of the law upon their hearts. The image of God would be imbedded within their mind, body and soul. Much of the teaching was oral; but the youth also learned to read the Hebrew writings; and the parchment rolls of the Old Testament Scriptures were open to their study.

In the days of Christ the town or city that did not provide for the religious instruction of the young was regarded as under the curse of God. Yet the teaching had become formal and tradition had in a great degree supplanted the Scriptures. True education would lead the youth to "seek the Lord, if happily they might seek after Him, and find Him." Acts17:27. But the Jewish teachers gave their attention to matters of ceremony. The mind was crowded with material that was worthless to the learner, and that would not be recognized in the higher school of the courts. The experience which is obtained through a personal acceptance of God's word had no place in the educational system. The students found no quiet hours to spend with God, as they would not hear GOD speaking to their hearts. In their search for knowledge, they would turn away from the wisdom of GOD. The service of God was neglected and the principles of the law were absence. The superior education was the greatest hindrance to real development under the training of the rabbis repressed ways of the youth. Their minds became cramped and narrow. The child Jesus did not receive instruction in the synagogue schools. His mother was His first human teacher. By way of the scrolls of the prophets His mother spoke and He learned of the heavenly things. The very words which Christ Himself had spoken to Moses for Israel He was now taught at His mother's knee. As He advanced from childhood to youth, He did not seek the schools of the rabbis. He did not need the education from those sources, for God was His instructor.

The question asked during the Savior's ministry, "How has this man become learned, having never educated?" does that indicate that Jesus was unable to read, or merely that He had not received a rabbinical education. John 7:15. Since He gained knowledge as we may do, His intimate acquaintance with the Scriptures show how diligently His early years were given to the study of God's word. And spread out before Him was the great created works of God. He who had made all things studied the lessons which His own hand had written in earth, sea and sky.

The Child, The Teen, The Adult

Apart from the unholy ways of the world, He gathered stores of scientific knowledge through nature. He studied the life of plants, animals, and the life of man. From His earliest years He was possessed of one purpose; He lived to bless others. He saw the resources in nature ways and means flashed into His mind as He studied plant life and animal life. Continually He drew from things seen illustrated by which to present the living oracles of God. The parables by which, during His ministry, He loved to teach His lessons of truth show how open His Spirit was to the influences of nature, and how He had gathered the spiritual teaching from the surroundings of His daily life. The significance of the word and works of God was unfolded. He was trying to understand the reason of the things of this world. Heavenly beings were His attendants, and the culture of holy thoughts. From the first dawning of intelligence He was constantly growing in spiritual grace and knowledge of truth. Every child may gain knowledge as Jesus did as we try to become acquainted with our heavenly Father through His word, angels will draw near, our minds will be strengthened, and our characters will be elevated and refined. We shall become more like our Savior. As we behold the beautiful nature of our affections for God. The Spirit of GOD and the soul of man are invigorated by the "Infinite Communion with God" through prayer. The mental, moral faculties and the spiritual powers strengthen as we cultivate thoughts upon spiritual things. The life of Jesus was a life in harmony with God. While He was a child, He thought and spoke as a child; but no trace of sin marred the image of God within Him. Yet He was not exempt from temptation. The inhabitants of Nazareth were proverbial for their wickedness. The low estimate in which they were generally held is shown by Nathanael's question, "Can there any good thing come out of Nazareth?" John 1:46. Jesus was placed where His character would be tested. It was necessary for Him to be constantly on guard in order to preserve His purity. He was subject to all the conflicts which we have to meet, that He might be an example to us in childhood, youth, and manhood. Satan was unwearied in his efforts to overcome the Child of Nazareth. From His earliest years Jesus was guarded by heavenly angels, yet His life was one long struggle against the powers of darkness. Upon the earth one life free from the defilement of evil was an offense and a perplexity to the prince of darkness.

He left no means untried to ensnare Jesus. No child of humanity will ever be called to live a Holy life amid so fierce a conflict with temptation as was our Savior. Joseph and Mary the parents of Jesus were poor, and dependent upon their daily toil. He was familiar with poverty, self-denial, and privation. This experience was a safeguard to Christ. In His industrious life there were no idle moments to invite temptation. No aimless hours opened the way for corrupting associations. He closed the door to all temptation. Neither gain nor pleasure nor applause nor censure, could induce Him to consent to a wrong act. He was wise to discern evil, and strong to resist it. Christ was the only sinless one who ever dwelt on earth; yet for nearly thirty years He lived among the wicked inhabitants of Nazareth. This fact is a rebuke to those who think themselves dependent upon place, fortune, or prosperity, in order to live a blameless life. Temptation, poverty, adversity, is the very discipline needed to develop purity and firmness. Jesus lived in a peasant's home, and faithfully and cheerfully acted His part in bearing the burdens of the household. He had been the Commander of heaven, and angels had delighted to fulfill His word; now He was a willing servant, a loving, obedient son. He learned a trade, and with His own hands worked in the carpenter's shop with Joseph. In the simple garb of a common laborer He walked the streets of the little town, going to and returning from His humble work. He did not employ His divine power to lessen His burdens or to lighten His toil. As Jesus worked in childhood and youth, mind and body were developed. He did not use His physical powers recklessly, but in such a way as to keep them in health, that He might do the best work in every line. He was not willing to be defective, even in the handling of tools. He was perfect as a workman, as He was perfect in character. By His own example He taught that it is our duty to be industrious, that our work should be performed with exactness and thoroughness, and that such labor is honorable. The exercise that teaches the hands to be useful and trains the young to bear their share of life's burdens gives physical strength, and develops every faculty. All should find something to do that will be beneficial to their lives and helpful to others. God appointed work as a blessing, and only the diligent worker finds the true glory and joy of life. The approval of God rests with loving assurance upon children and youth who cheerfully take their part in the duties of the household, sharing the burdens of father and mother.

The Child, The Teen, The Adult

Such children will go out from the home to be powerful members of society. Throughout His life on earth, Jesus was an earnest and constant worker. He expected much; therefore He attempted much, as He entered into His ministry, He said, "I must work the works of Him that sent Me, while it is day: the night comes, when no man can work." John 9:4. Jesus did not denounce care and responsibility, as do many who profess to be His followers. It is because they seek to evade this discipline that so many are weak and inefficient. They may possess precious and admirable traits, but they are nerveless and almost useless when difficulties are to be met or obstacles surmounted. The energy and strength of character, manifested in Christ are to be developed in us, through the same discipline that He endured. And the grace that He received is for us. So long as He lived among men, our Savior lived out the life of the poor. He experience their cares and hardships, and could comfort and encourage all. Those who have a true conception of the teaching of Christ life will never feel that a distinction must be made between classes of people, which the rich are to be honored worthy above the poor. Jesus carried into His labor cheerfulness and teachings. It requires much patience and spirituality to bring Bible into the home life and into the workshop, to bear the strain of worldly business, and yet keep the eye single to the glory of God. This is where Christ was a helper. He was never as full of worldly care as to have no time or thought for heavenly things. Often He expressed the gladness of His heart by singing psalms and heavenly songs. Often the dwellers in Nazareth heard His voice rose in praise and thanksgiving to God. He held communion with heaven in song; and as His companions complained of weariness from labor, they were cheered by the sweet melody from His lips. His praise seemed to banish the evil angels, and, like incense, fill the place with fragrance. The minds of His hearers were carried away from their earthly exile, to the heavenly home. Jesus was the fountain of healing mercy for the world; and through all those secluded years at Nazareth, His life flowed out in currents of sympathy and tenderness. The aged, the sorrowing, and the sin-burdened, the children at play in their innocent joy, the little creatures of the groves, the patient beasts of burden,--all were happier for His presence. He whose word of power upheld the worlds would stoop to relieve a wounded bird. There was nothing beneath His notice, nothing to which He disdained to minister.

Thus as He grew in wisdom and stature, Jesus increased in favor with God and man. He drew the sympathy of all hearts by showing Himself capable of sympathizing with all. The atmosphere of hope and courage that surrounded Him made Him a blessing in every home. And often in the synagogue on the Sabbath day He was called upon to read the lesson from the prophets, and the hearts of the hearers thrilled as a new light shone out from the familiar words of the sacred text. Jesus shunned being seen during all the years of His stay in Nazareth. He made no exhibition of the express power of the miracles, signs and healing. He sought no high position and assumed no religious titles. His quiet, simple life, and even the silence of the Scriptures concerning His early years, teaches an important lesson. The more quiet and simple the life of the child,--the more free from artificial excitement, and the more in harmony with nature,--the more favorable is it to physical and mental vigor and to spiritual strength. Jesus is our example; it is in His home life that He is the pattern for all children and youth. The Savior condescended to poverty, which He might teach how humbly one may walk with God. He lived to please, honor, and glorify His Father in the common things of life. His work began in consecrating the lowly trade of the craftsmen who toil for their daily bread. He was doing God's service just as much when laboring at the carpenter's bench as when working miracles for the multitude. And every youth who follows Christ's example of faithfulness and obedience in His lowly home may claim those words spoken of Him by the Father through the Holy Spirit, "Behold My Servant, whom I uphold; Mine Elect, in whom My soul delighted." Isa. 42:1.The New Testament binds a great responsibility on children when it says in Ephesians 6, verses 1-3, "Children obey your parents in the Lord: for this is right. Honor thy father and mother; (which is the first commandment with promise ;) that it may be well with you, and you may live long on the earth". The key words are "honor" and "obey". There is no time limit on this. God does not free a child from this responsibility simply because he has now gone to college or is married. A child in the earliest years of adulthood makes a tragic mistake by neglecting his parents. It is necessary that we say something about the word "obey". Children are to obey their parents "in the Lord". One must never forget that his allegiance to God comes before any man. That includes government, companions and parents.

The Child, The Teen, The Adult

The early apostles expressed it well when they were commanded not to preach in the name of Christ. They responded by saying in Acts 5, verse 29, "We ought to obey God rather than men". The term "obey your parents" indicates that the parents have laid down some laws or provided some instruction to guide the children. This is what is meant by the wise man when he said in Proverbs 22, verse 6, "Train up a child in the way he should go: and when he is old he will not depart from it". It is understood then that the law is to be obeyed by the child is that which will make him a fine, decent, responsible person. Instructions of parents should be revered by children beyond the parent's death. No time limit then on "Children obey your parents in the Lord" Ephesians 6:1. The other word that stands out so predominantly in the children's responsibility to their parents is the word "honor". The Bible says in Ephesians 6, verse 2, "Honor your father and mother". This responsibility deals with the child's attitude and respect toward the parents. The word honor means "High regard of great respect given", "Something done or given as a token of respect". The home for centuries has provided an environment for one to learn all of the ABC's of Christian living. It is in the home that seeds of character can be sown and given an opportunity to flourish. The great principles of God are to be taught, practiced and cultivated in the home. The child who has learned to honor parents can then effectively show high regard toward his fellow man. He later can easily show respect for a companion and his own children. It is important that we pause to say that parents have the responsibility to provide the proper atmosphere in the home so that the child can develop an appreciation for law and order given by parents. Such an environment will cause children to rise up and greatly respect the parent. The example of parents sets the stage for loving one another, far more reaching in the heart and life-pattern of the child. When a child cannot see parents love, respect and honor one another, it is extremely difficult for him to rise above this obstacle and honor those that do not honor themselves. Remember, in order to manifest honor towards others, you must love and respect oneself. Christ provides us with an example in all things. Having returned from the visit to the city of Jerusalem at the age of 12, the Bible says that Christ, "was subject unto them: but his mother kept all these sayings in her heart. And Jesus increased in wisdom and in stature and in favor with God and man" Luke 2, verses 51, 52. Christ was obedient to his parents.

His affection and respect for his mother was manifested from the cross. He was concerned about her care and well-being. He gave this responsibility to the beloved Apostle John (John 19:25-27). You shall always be children in the eyes of your parents and in the eyes of the Lord. Your response to the commandment, "Obey your parents" and "Honor thy father and thy mother", will be a pretty good yardstick measuring how well you will obey your Lord and give Him honor through faithful worship. The child's responsibility is a lifetime achievement, an achievement that will be richly blessed in all walks of life. In the words of Ephesians Chapter 6, it is the first commandment with promise. Good parents refuse to leave their children at the mercy of their own folly. Exerting every effort to prepare their children for successful living, they teach them the needful skills of self-control, respect for authority, consideration for others, and submission to God. This training involves teaching, leading, correcting. In a word, this training involves discipline. First, effective discipline is consistent, but it is next to impossible to be perfectly consistent. Personal feelings often spoil our efforts to be consistent. One day because mother has a headache, the child must toe the mark. The following day when everything is going well, the child can get away with anything. Fire always burns, and children learn not to touch it because it is consistently hot. A parent's "no" has meaning only if that parent is consistent, never permitting the child to ignore it. Effective discipline is positive and discipline is not all negative. The steady patience of a positive parent can shape strong character in a child. God gave high compliments to Abraham when he said of him, "I know him, that he will command his children and his household after him, and they shall keep the way of the Lord", Genesis 18:19. Abraham led by character, Joshua admonished Israel, "Choose you this day whom you will serve," then he added the strong words, "but as for me and my house, we will serve the Lord," Joshua 24:15. He was a successful disciplinarian of others because he was successful in self-discipline. Planting Bible principles in the heart of a child is the most reliable insurance a parent can have against disobedience and rebellion. By the time a child reaches school age, he may be spending the majority of his waking hours away from parental influence. If those first six years have been used by Godly parents to instill an awareness of God's presence and to develop a sense of right and wrong, the child is much less vulnerable to undesirable influences.

The Child, The Teen, The Adult

The child who has been taught respect for parental authority is more likely to respect the authority of civil law and of God. He also needs to learn the discipline of work. Learning to be a responsible, productive member, of the family is important. Picking up toys and putting away clothes helps prepare the child for the responsibilities of adult life. Effective discipline is individualized and wise parents do not compare one child to another. Children are individuals, each with strengths and weaknesses. They Find security in being loved, accepted and even when the child is punished, he must sense that it is because he is loved. (Hebrews 12:5-6) Proper discipline must be individualized and each situation must be seen from the proper view point before issuing mandates. Parents should respect a child's right to express themselves, being courteous and considerate of his feelings. This is living the golden rule of Matthew 7:12. Effective discipline is rewarding and there may be times when discipline is met by obstinacy and parents may be tempted to become soft and permissive, but what is actually needed at this time is an added measure of firmness. This temptation must be rejected if the rewards of parenthood are to be realized as seeing children grow into Christ-like living; productive adults are a reward of affective discipline. The Bible says that children are a heritage of the Lord, like arrows in the hand of a warrior, are the sons of one's youth; Happy is the man who's quiver is full of them, he has not been put to shame, Psalms 127:3-5. Solomon said, "Train up a child in the way he should go, and when he is old he will not depart from it" Proverbs 22:6. The word discipline derives from the Greek word which means "to teach". Our reducing of this good word to denote only the punishment of those who do wrong is a mistake. And the widely held notion that he is the best parent who most sternly and severely punishes his child for wrong-doing is a more serious mistake. Wrong-doing results in harm and is therefore to be avoided. This is a lesson every child should learn and it is necessary for a child to feel something of the ill that results from his wrong attitudes and acts. In infancy and early childhood, when reasoning powers are limited, the child may be able to understand this only when his misdeeds are immediately and sharply related to something that pains him. It is here, no doubt, that the proverbial "rod" must be applied to prevent bad attitudes and acts from becoming habits (Proverbs 13:24; 23:13).

But true discipline not only emphasizes the ill that comes from harmful acts; it also hastens to show the good effects that come from good acts and attitudes. And when the child's powers of reason are not well developed to see such natural, good effects, the wise and thoughtful parent will reward the child's good deeds with immediate and pleasant things. True discipline is positive, as well as negative. Jesus' parable of the man from whom the demon was driven is excellent illustration (Luke 11:23-26). The demons wandered in dry places and found no home. They eventually came back to their former home to find that it was swept and garnished - but still empty! Immediately demons that had been met in wanderings and were invited for reinforcement as an empty heart of the man he had formerly inhabited. The man's last state was worse than the first! That "discipline" which is concerned only with removing evil is doomed to fail. It may result in making a child good, but good for nothing! True discipline not only guards, but guides. It overcomes evil with good. Timothy was wisely disciplined in that in his childhood his mind was filled with the knowledge of the sacred Scripture (11 Timothy 3:15). Jesus at twelve years of age was committed to His father's business (Luke 2:49). Paul refers to an attitude of some teachers who multiply rules such as "do not touch, do not taste, do not handle", which, he says, have a show of wisdom in will-worship but have no value against the indulgence of the flesh (Colossians 2:20-23). True discipline is not the one who knows only the don'ts but the one who accept instructions and practice the dos. Effective discipline consists of words and acts of correction; it involves instruction to good deeds and thoughts, the most effective discipline is love and patients in all things. The teachers who are most sure of success are those whose love and patience inspire their discipline. Those parents who demonstrate daily and fully in righteousness, patience, unselfish service both in and out of the home, are those who truly discipline their children! Teenager to express freedom's first limitation are more generally, "Is this good for mans soul?" Humans are not bodies that have souls; rather they are spirits that will live as long as God exists. God's limitation on our freedom is that we must not be mastered by, or brought under, the power of the things we do. Jesus said that no man can serve two masters. Thus, servants of Christ must never serve other things. But you say, "I will not be slave to anyone or anything, I shall be free".

The Child, The Teen, The Adult

This is a popular myth; no human has ever lived who wasn't mastered by someone or something. It might have been kin, or boss, sexual drives, lust for wealth, liquor, cigarettes, or drugs. Everybody has a master of some kind. It is better to be slave to the master over heaven and earth than to our own selfishness, indulgences, and bad habits. How free is the alcoholic? How free is the slave of the desire for material gain, surrounded by wealth, yet desperately unhappy having no real purpose in life? Mankind can stand great pain, suffering and privation. Mankind cannot stand life without meaning or without purpose. Materialism and other modern concepts confuse young people. Many don't know what they should believe, and their lives have become without purpose or meaning. This is one reason why suicide among our young, ages 15 through 23, are the greatest cause of death, second only to accidents. We must choose which master we will serve (we will serve someone or something). To be free we must choose our activities to include only those that serve Jesus and His kingdom. In so doing, our lives will have clear meaning and purpose. God directs our activities to be constructive, that is, they must edify, or build-up, both those around us, and ourselves. This is so because freedom is also a social dimension. You cannot take another's goods because this conflicts with his right to keep them. You cannot speed on the highways because this interferes with the rights of others to travel safely. The notion of absolute freedom is an absurdity. No one has ever been absolutely free to do everything he might wish to do. All of us are bounded and constrained by the needs and rights of others and by our own limitations. We easily fall for the cheap solution, "I can do what I want as long as nobody gets hurt". How do you judge who gets hurt? What is hurt? How much hurt is permissible? Can you speed ahead on the highway squandering fuel without consuming from those you have passed? Will they get to their destination if the service station's allocation ends with you? Is the decision made by two young people in a moment of passion theirs to alone to make? Are their families implicated? Is the child, unaffected? We can do what we want, but it must be beneficial to all, it must serve the true Lord of us all, and it must be constructive for all. Adolescence is a time when the individual questions "Do I like myself?" "What am I going to do for the rest of my life?", "What are my good qualities?", "How should I change?", or "What do other people think of me?" It is a time of growing.

The Kingdom Culture Community

The Teenager is leaving childhood where he was dependent upon his parents to direct him, to provide for him, and to make his decisions for him. He is becoming an adult capable of caring for him and, in turn, being responsible to and for others. There are certain activities in which our society generally expects teenagers to participate. One of these is dating. Traditionally, children worked until their parents decided that it was time for them to marry, the parents then selected the mate, and the new home was begun. Our society feels it better for those whose lives are most directly involved to make the important decision as to who they will marry. Accordingly, dating allows young people to be exposed to different personalities and to judge (to some extent) the effects that the various personality traits might have upon a lifelong relationship. Dating lets boys and girls see these traits at work in a variety of situations. This is important experience and education. Also, dating lets the young person observes himself, or herself, under diverse situations, and it's important that each person get to know himself very well. There are also other reasons for dating, such as having a good time, being socially accepted, and just being with friends. Dating is fun. It is a time to get to know another person more completely, a time to share ideas, plans and hopes, a time to do interesting things with someone special. When a teenager begins to date, he is uncertain about many things. That very first date causes both excitement and anxious moments. One of the most important decisions a teenager will make is choosing the people he will date. "Do not be misleading: Bad company corrupts good character" (NIV), I Corinthians 15:33 and in Psalm 1:1, "Blessed is the man who walks not in the counsel of the wicked" (RSV). We easily recognize the influence of our friends in our lives. They influence us in many ways that are more important than just clothes and hair length. If our friends use drugs, obscene language, or engage in premarital sex; how much harder will it be for you to remain acceptable to God? II Corinthians 6:14-16 says, "Do not be yoked together with unbelievers. For what do righteousness and wickedness have in common? What does a believer have in common with an unbeliever? What agreement is there between the temple of God and idols? For we are the temple of the living God", if we form close personal relationships with persons whose moral standards are opposed to the teachings of Jesus', are we not endangering our inheritance of the Kingdom?

The Child, The Teen, The Adult

Sometimes dating situations develop because of the places selected and the type of recreation chosen. If we choose a date who shares our moral standards, we have made a good beginning. However, remember that both you and your date are human with normal male and female sexual drives. These are God given, they are normal, and they can bring much joy and fulfillment. But remember, God placed very specific restrictions upon when the sexual drive may be fulfilled. I Corinthians 6:9-10 says, "Don't you know that the wicked will not inherit the kingdom of God? Do not be deceived: Neither the sexually immoral nor idolaters nor adulterers nor male prostitutes nor homosexual offenders nor thieves nor the greedy nor drunkards nor slanders nor swindlers will inherit the kingdom of God". (NIV) If on the majority of your dates you are alone, and you go to cozy, intimate places, are you not making it easier for Devil to manipulate your thinking to do wrong? Time and familiarity with another person can slowly but very surely break down our defenses. It is a valuable guideline to consider dating as a hands-off activity. Once a boy and girl begin to touch, feel and caress one another, the stop signs become blurred and convictions lose their strength. Remember that under conditions of mutual respect, the boy will never try to take advantage of the girl; neither will the girl tempt the boy by thoughtless dress or action which will tend to arouse his natural desire. Mutual consideration is a two way street. In conclusion it should be pointed out that dating is an important, but a small part of a teenager's total life, just as the icing is an important, but a small part of the cake. Dating too often (or for too many hours) is like a cake that is all icing. Keep dating activities in balance; do not let dating interfere with your duties to God, to family, to school, or to self. If parental influence is not great enough to maintain control of the child through these powerful group influences and if normal group behavior includes immorality, trouble will almost surely come to your child soon. It is not without obvious reason that the Bible warns against certain association, saying, "Be not deceived, evil companionships corrupt good morals". I Corinthians 15:33. The old-fashioned requirement of having your child end his outside activities at a reasonable hour is quite valid and applicable today. Unlimited time for amusement often leads to poor performance at school, at work, and at home. The family that waits up for a late comer will also suffer for lack of rest. Too, the younger children will clamor for the same unlimited privilege.

The Kingdom Culture Community

You have the right and the duty to control your children, for the Bible says that, "He that provides not for his own is worse than an infidel" I Timothy 5:8. Providing for your children includes love, direction, discipline, and control, as well as the physical necessities of life. We do not advise an ever-abiding, all-prevailing control of the child. Parents must not stifle the growth of the child by extreme-control; as the child matures, parental control should be gradually released. It is indeed a fine line that parents must walk; between too much and too little control - and it requires kind of judgment. Early training of the child is important. Obedience to parents must be developed early from infancy to adult teens. It is important to maintain respect with your children early in their lives. Fear of GOD and honor to the parent can be maintained throughout their lives into adulthood. Young people leave home for a variety of reasons. The most usual is that they grow up and leave their parents to be on their own, and to start a home of their own. Sometimes children leave because of conflict within the home. Whatever the reason, when you leave home, time should be taken for deep consideration and for prayers for guidance. Now, when you are starting your new life, you will have two major obstacles to overcome if you are to maintain a high moral standard or to improve a lower one. The greatest obstacle is yourself for the Bible tells us that, "The Spirit is willing, but the flesh is weak" (Mark 14:38). With no one to awaken you and make you get up and attend worship, it is all too easy to neglect this duty. Without outside guidance, you will often be tempted to neglect your studies or fail to report to work. A mature person has the initiative to stick to a job until it is finished. Once you have established a path to follow through careful thought, prayers, and counsel, do not allow your friends to become an obstacle. Do not let them do your thinking for you; do your own thinking. Friends are people with likes and dislikes similar to those of your own. You share your deeper thoughts with them and you care about them and they care about you. Obviously, they way they think and the things they do greatly influence your outlook and activities. If you choose friends of good moral and spiritual outlook they will help strengthen you. If your friends are people who disrespect God, their parents, and the law, it will be exceedingly difficult for you to avoid disgrace and a turbulent life. For this reason "Evil companions corrupt good morals". I Corinthians 15:33.

The Child, The Teen, The Adult

A true friend really cares for your spiritual, emotional, and physical well-being. One who calls himself a friend but who would influence you into evil thoughts and actions is really a selfish person wanting only to find someone who will condone his foolish sinful life. Choose your friends wisely. Some of the world's greatest accomplishments have been done by young men and women. Alexander the Great became king before he was thirty years old. Some of the great works of Shelley, Byron, Keats, Chopin, and Mozart were composed when they were teenagers. Hitler and Mussolini built their power on the dedication and energy of young people. Today, Communists make their strongest sales pitch to youth, because they know of the influence and dedication of the young. Now, much of the mission work of the church is being done by young adults. And the church needs consecrated young people. Times are perilous and our cause is the greatest that the world has ever known. The very hope of the human race lies in wise youth committed to high principles. Young people need the church they need Christ. Those who are indifferent to the way of the Lord are inviting sorrow on their lives and souls. Jesus says to young and old alike, "If any man will come after me, let him deny himself, and take up his cross, and follow me" (Mark 8:34)."Hear, my son, your father's instruction And do not forsake your mother's teaching; indeed, they are a graceful wreath to your head and ornaments about your neck." Proverbs 1:8-9

"A wise son accepts his father's discipline, but a scoffer does not listen to rebuke." Proverbs 13:1

"A fool rejects his father's discipline, but he who regards reproof is sensible." Proverbs 15:5

"Listen to your father who begot you, and do not despise your mother when she is old." Proverbs 23:22

"He who keeps the law is a discerning son, but he who is a companion of gluttons humiliates his father." Proverbs 28:7

"There is a kind of man who curses his father and does not bless his mother." Proverbs 30:11

"Remember also your Creator in the days of your youth, before the evil days come and the years draw near when you will say, "I have no delight in them";" Ecclesiastes 12:1

"Children, obey your parents in the Lord, for this is right. Honor your father and mother (which is the first commandment with a promise), so that it may be well with you, and that you may live long on the earth. Fathers, do not provoke your children to anger, but bring them up in the discipline and instruction of the Lord." Ephesians 6:1-4 "Fathers, do not exasperate your children, so that they will not lose heart." Colossians 3:21"But if any widow has children or grandchildren, they must first learn to practice piety in regard to their own family and to make some return to their parents; for this is acceptable in the sight of God." 1 Timothy 5:4 ""If any man has a stubborn and rebellious son who will not obey his father or his mother, and when they chastise him, he will not even listen to them, then his father and mother shall seize him, and bring him out to the elders of his city at the gateway of his hometown. "They shall say to the elders of his city, 'This son of ours is stubborn and rebellious, he will not obey us, and he is a glutton and a drunkard.' "Then all the men of his city shall stone him to death; so you shall remove the evil from your midst, and all Israel will hear of it and fear." Deuteronomy 21:18-21 "The eye that mocks a father and scorns a mother, the ravens of the valley will pick it out, and the young eagles will eat it." Proverbs 30:17"'If there is anyone who curses his father or his mother, he shall surely be put to death; he has cursed his father or his mother, his blood guiltiness is upon him." Leviticus 20:9

The Adult

According to the Word of God, a person becomes an adult when they reach the age of 20 (twenty). The word "adult," however, is not found in the Bible. "Adults" are referred to as "men" or "women." An "adult" is simply defined as "a person who is not a child." A person who is under the age of 20 (twenty) is a child. The Bible refers to people from conception through the age of 19 as children. God refers to children in the womb as "children"--not "embryos" (children from conception through 8 weeks), or "fetuses" (children 8 weeks through birth), or "tissue."

The Child, The Teen, The Adult

God also explains that babies in the womb cannot do good or evil. Romans 9:11 says, "For the children being not yet born, neither having done any good or evil..."The Bible also uses various words to describe children, some of which differentiate between the ages of them: babes, babies, infants, boys, girls, little ones, children, youths, etc. A boy is a male under the age of 20. A man is a male age 20 or over. A girl is a female under the age of 20. A woman is a female age 20 or over. God pronounced judgment on all the Israelites who were 20 years old or older (except for Joshua and Caleb and their families) because they had refused to believe Him even after all the signs and wonders that He had done in Egypt and the wilderness on their way to the Promised Land. They were sentenced to wander in the wilderness for 40 years until they dropped dead. Numbers 14:29-30 says: "Your carcasses shall fall in this wilderness; and all that were numbered of you, according to your whole number, from twenty years old and upward which have murmured against me. Doubtless ye shall not come into the land, concerning which I swore to make you dwell therein, save Caleb the son of Jephunneh, and Joshua the son of Nun." The Bible goes on to say in Numbers 14:31-33: "But your little ones, which ye said should be a prey, them will I bring in, and they shall know the land which ye have despised. But as for you, your carcasses, they shall fall in this wilderness. And your children shall wander in the wilderness forty years, and bear your whoredoms, until your carcasses be wasted in the wilderness." We see from this last passage of scripture that "little ones" is used interchangeably with and means the same thing as "children." God said that all the Israelites would have to spend forty years wandering in the wilderness until all the people who were 20 years old or older--at the time of this pronouncement by God--died. All the people who were not yet 20 years old, who had not yet reached their 20th birthday, the "little ones," the "children," would be allowed to live. However, they would have to wander for 40 years in the wilderness before they would be allowed to enter into the Promised Land. We see here the difference that God makes between people who are 20 and over, and people who are under 20. Without a doubt, there were numerous teenagers and other children who were just as sinful and murmured and complained just as much as their parents. But God did not sentence them to die, as He did the adults. The reason is that God does not hold children to the same accountability as He does adults.

The Kingdom Culture Community

I Corinthians 13:11 says: "When I was a child, I spoke as a child, I understood as a child, I thought as a child: but when I became a man, I put away childish things." Children--people 19 years old and younger--think and understand like children. There are a few exceptions. Occasionally you may meet a teenager who is very mature for their age, and by the age of 17, 18, or 19 may seem to act like an adult. But this is very rare, and they probably do not act like an adult in every way. But because they are children, and they think and act and understand like children, God does not hold them fully accountable for their actions as He does adults. God holds adults--those 20 years of age and older--fully accountable for their own actions. But with children, God holds them accountable on a sliding scale. A baby, of course, has no accountability for his actions. He does not even know what he is doing. But as that baby grows, God begins to hold that child more and more accountable for his actions until the time when he reaches the age of 20 and is fully accountable for his actions. This is why God allowed the children to live and enter the Promised Land, but He sentenced the adults to die in the wilderness. Someone may ask, "Why didn't God just strike all the adults dead on the spot and allow the children to enter the Promised Land without having to wander 40 years in the wilderness?" The answer is pretty obvious. If all the adults were struck dead by God instantly, there would be no adults left to raise the remaining children. At this time there were approximately 1.2 million adult Israelites. Exodus 12:37 and Numbers 11:21 explain that there were approximately 600,000 men. Figuring approximately the same number of women, you come to about 1,200,000 adults. If you guesstimate how many children there were, you will come to a number far above 2 million children! This number not only would include the teenagers and younger children, but it would also include numerous infants who were being breastfed at the time. God was not about to kill off the parents and leave over 2 million children orphans. However, before Moses interceded for the children of Israel (Numbers 14:13-19), God was going to wipe them all out--including the children (Numbers 14:11-12). You will also notice in the Bible that whenever God numbered the people, whether it was for a census, for military reasons, or whatever, He counted the people who were 20 years old and older.

The Child, The Teen, The Adult

(Exodus 38:26; Numbers chapter 1; II Chronicles 31:17; Ezra 3:8) This is significant because the age of 20 signifies adulthood. Jesus passed by, He saw a man which was blind from his birth. His disciples asked Him, saying, Master, who did sin, this man, or his parents, that he was born blind? Jesus answered, neither this man sinned, nor his parents..." what Christ is showing us, is that this person had been blind for at least 20 (twenty) years, because he had been blind from his birth and was now an adult. It explains how Jesus healed the man so that he could see. The man's parents said: "...he is of age; ask him: he shall speak for himself." We see that a "man" is of age and can speak for himself. This would also be true of a "woman." A "woman" is a person who is of age and can speak for herself. In other words, a person must be 20 years of age to speak for him or herself. If a person is not yet 20, they are under the authority of their parents, and their parents speak for them. Understanding that a person ceases being a child and becomes an adult at age 20 is very important to the Christian. The Word of God commands parents to discipline their children, and commands children to obey their parents in the Lord. (Proverbs 22:6, 15; Ephesians 6:1). If a Christian does not know at what age a person becomes an adult, then how would a parent know when his child is too old to be disciplined? When would a child know that he is no longer a child and does not have to obey his parents anymore? Surely, we cannot rely on the governments of the world to tell us! And different governmental bodies set different ages for "adulthood." So if a person of a particular age is standing within the borders of one government, they would be classified as an "adult." But if they walk a few steps into the borders of another government, they are then classified as a "child." Does a person really change from an "adult" into a "child" because they cross over a border into another government's jurisdiction? And when they walk back within the borders of the former government, does the person then change back into an "adult?" Some governments, like ours here in the United States, say that at certain ages people are adults in some areas, but yet are still classified as children in others! For instance, our government says that 18 year olds are adults as far as smoking cigarettes is concerned, but are children as far as drinking alcohol is concerned until they reach the age of 21! Different countries of the world (and different states here in the United States) consider people to be adults at different ages for marriage purposes.

The Kingdom Culture Community

Sometimes males are classified as adults at one age and females are classified as adults at another age! This can be contrary to the Word of God and is just plain confusion but Paul when speaking of the government says in GODs word to obey the law of the land. As Christians, we are to live by the Word of God, but if there is a conflict with the laws teach man Gods laws, that we can obey God rather than conflict with man." (Acts 5:29) Ephesians 6:1 says: "Children, obey your parents in the Lord: for this is right." This refers to children, who are still children--that is, it is referring to children who have not yet reached their 20th birthday. For when they reach their 20th birthday they are no longer children and no longer in "obedience to their parents in the Lord." But at that point respecting the parents for throughout life as long as the parents are still living! Exodus 20:12 says: "Honor your father and your mother: that your days may be long upon the land which the Lord your God gives you." Honoring is NOT the same thing as obeying. Honoring one's parents is giving them the respect that is due them as parents--even if they were and are bad parents. For example, you would NEVER call your parents by their first names! You would NOT get into a shouting match with them.

You would calmly disagree, if you disagreed with them, even if they were going off on you. And you may have to walk away, but you would do it respectfully after saying good-bye. It may even be that because your parents are so bad, you cannot see or talk to them--but you still are respectful to them because the Bible says that you must honor them all the days of your life. Obeying one's parents means to do as your parents tell you to do. If it conflict with what Gods Word tells you then inform your parents in a respectful manner. Some parents teach their children to steal and lie and to do other immoral acts. As a Christian child, you would not obey your parents if they told you to do things like that. The Bible says to obey them "in the Lord." This means to obey them as long as it is in line with what the Lord says. However, once you reach the age of 20, "Children, obey your parents in the Lord: for this is right." no longer applies to you, because you are no longer a child. By the same token, parents are commanded to bring their children up in the nurture and admonition of the Lord (Ephesians 6:4). They are commanded to train up their children in the way that they should go (Proverbs 22:6). They are commanded to drive foolishness from the hearts of their children (Proverbs 22:15).

The Child, The Teen, The Adult

This only applies to the parents and their children while the children are still children--that is, while the children are under the age of 20. For once a child turns 20, he is no longer a child, but has become an adult.

CHAPTER IV

The Purpose for Sex

God created us with the desire for sex, and we ought to understand his design that was meant for us in our relationships with others about sex. Christians absolutely need to seek God's purpose in this area of their lives. God created us male and female and because of that we will be attracted to one another, why? We are the opposite sex and it is a part of creation that woman was made for man as a part of creation. But we must learn to control our desires because having sex, and even the desire for sex with someone outside of marriage is not God's plan. God created man in his own image; in the image of God he created him; male and female he created them. God blessed them and said to them: Be Fruitful and Multiply, and Replenish the Earth (Genesis 1:26-30). God intends for a married man and woman to have sexual relations for the purpose of replenishing the earth within the confines of marriage. God wants us to have sex so we will bring forth more children into the world for him and to teach and train our children up in the wisdom of God! Had Adam and Eve decided to not have sex and have children then essentially they would have been rebelling against God's purpose and instruction. Controlling our Sex Drive, even though sex is good, it must be controlled! As we look at society we see many uncontrolled desires and sex drives running amok causing much harm and danger. People blame God for plagues and diseases but these things are caused from your own rebelliousness toward GOD! When we choose to disobey God's commands things happens because of our own foolish choices, as the bible tells us "There are ways that seems right to a man but in the end, it leads to death. Prov. 14:12. Sex outside of marriage may seem so right to one but it is against the Law of GOD, you break the law you automatically start the process of punishment brought on by the hand of GOD.

As with anything in life we must control it, so it will not overtake our lives and cause spiritual and emotional turmoil for us. We must control our sex drive, lest we hurt others, damage our relationships and ourselves, and sin against God. If we don't control our appetite for food we become overweight and sick. In the same way if we don't control our appetite for sex it will control us and tempt us into immoral acts of lust. That lust will lead to other things that many are not prepared to handle. More dangerous if this thing lead to danger for all parties involved. Did you know that your bodies are members of Christ himself? Shall I then take the members of Christ and unite them with a prostitute? Never! Do you know that he who unites himself with a prostitute is one with her in body? For it is said, "The two will becomes one flesh." But he who unites himself with lord is one with him in spirit. Paul uses this incident with the Corinthian church immorality ways and means to bring out GODs certification in marriage. GOD certifies a union by way of sexual relations between a man and a woman. It is the law of the land that certifies a marriage by way of documentation such as a marriage license. Does GOD recognize the law of the land? Absolutely, Paul speaks of in the book of it in Rom. 13:1, "Everyone must submit himself to the governing authorities, for there is no authority except that which God has established. The authorities that exist have been established by GOD." God says that sex is a beautiful and healthy part of life when it is between a married man and woman. But he also lets us know that the sex drive must be used for his purpose

Fornication is sexual intercourse between two unmarried people "the defrauding of each other". Many of us think about things with a different perspective than what many have been brought up to believe, sex without any real intention for marriage is a deception and is morally wrong. This is why God calls fornication a sin. Sex outside of the boundaries of marriage will lead the hand of GOD against you. God does not want to see us heart broken or sick from disease because we gave into sexual immorality. God loves us and wants what is best for us, to reserve having sex until we are married.

The Purpose for Sex

"For this is the will of God, that you should be sanctified: that you should avoid sexual immorality; that each of you should learn to control his own body in a way that is holy and honorable, not in passionate lust like the heathen, who do not know GOD; and that in this matter no one should wrong his brother or take advantage of him. The Lord will punish men for all such sins, as we have already told you and warned you. For GOD did not call us to be impure, but to live a holy life. (1 Thessalonians 4:3-7). Marriage is the only intended purpose for sex. Anything else perverts and distorts sexual relations and the mind, body and spirit of a person. God created sex for sexual enjoyment in marriage. The bottom line is our sex drive was created for the purpose of procreation and sexual fulfillment between a husband and a wife! Realizing the proper use of our sex drive is the first step in controlling it. Then the Lord GOD made a woman from the rib he had taken out of the man, and he brought her to the man. Then man said, "This is now bone of my bones and flesh of my flesh; she shall be called woman, for she was taken out of man." For this reason a man will leave his father and mother and be united to his wife, and they will become one flesh. The man and his wife were both naked, and they felt no shame. (Genesis 2:23-25). The sex drive is not dirty, until we choose to abuse it. The sex drive is not sinful, until we choose to abuse it. Our sex drive is an awesome gift from God that should be used to honor and glorify God with by bringing forth children, and for our own enjoyment in marriage. The institution of marriage allows the lawful sexual union between male and female in the eyes of God and society. Since both, male and female should dedicate their lives to the Will of God and the great struggle in the journey of the meeting with God, the great struggle of the union between the two, then the pleasure derived from sex is Divinely given to enhance the union as well as to re-charge the electrical energy of the male and the female that they might continue the great journey and struggle of life. These two, properly motivated, allows the sexual union to be a life-giving experience not only in procreation and continuance of the life of the species, but, it is invigorating as well as life giving to the marriage and the struggle of these two to become as one. To look at marriage as only the legalization of the sex act is to put our minds on a level that will not bring the best out of the experience. To become extreme in our view that the sex act is only for procreation and not meant by God to give pleasure to married couples is a view that is not in accord with the Will, Plan and Purpose of God.

The Kingdom Culture Community

These pleasure centers in the human being, used properly and in accord with the Will of God, brings comfort, ease, consolation, rest, reward and joy to the souls that are working hard to fulfill their Divine duty and obligation.

What is the purpose of sex in marriage?
1. Procreation of human species.
2. Reward the struggle of the two to become one with the joy of the pleasure of each other's complimentary nature.
3. To give rest, relaxation and new energy to the male to continue the great mission of being producer of mastering the earth and its laws as we strives to become one who stands in the place of God at his level of development. The female in energizing the male and giving him this comfort, consolation; giving him peace and quiet of mind as a rest period between struggle is also satisfied and is pleased because she has given rest to him to work for God, her and the family. Therefore, she is rested in herself. This is the Divine Purpose of Sex in Marriage. Satan, however, has taken this natural gift of God and made mischief with it causing us to go after pleasure without struggle; without the burden or responsibility of being what God created us to be. We have become pleasure seekers without responsibility and misusing our pleasure centers thus becoming slaves of pleasure. This has given rise to the misuse of women and the misuse of what God gave them for the man so that she becomes a prostitute – sex for hire, he becomes a pimp – using her and the need of the male for pleasure as a means of livelihood. The lust for pleasure is causing the abuse of children, male and female, and the misuse of our bodies. As a result, we are living in a morally degenerate world. We are paying the price for this moral degeneracy through the plague of AIDS and sexually transmitted diseases, which produce the destruction of the male and female and the destruction of our future. This is why we must return to God and seek to know His purpose for what He created and use everything of creation in accord with His purpose for it. Then, and only then, will we find the genuine peace, joy, and happiness that we seek. Psalms says, "Behold, how good and how pleasant it is for brethren to dwell together in unity!" Unity awards us another kind of pleasure. There is tremendous pleasure in being one with God. There is tremendous joy in knowing that we are pleasing in His sight.

The Purpose for Sex

Let us strive for the real pleasure of life that comes from duty to God through his Son Christ Jesus; duty to ourselves; duty to our mates; duty to our families; duty to our community. Let us seek real pleasure that comes when we know that we have struggled to obey God; we have struggled to bear the burden of the great responsibility that God has placed on our shoulders; we have accepted the difficulty factor of life knowing truly that after difficulty comes ease. What is marriage for? The answer that you'll get from children's stories is, "to live happily ever after." The answer we get from television and movies is, "to make your life miserable ever after." No two people get married in order to make themselves or each other miserable. They marry with optimism that life truly will be more meaningful and emotionally richer. Before the 1960"s, the divorce rate was a lot lower than it is today and most couples reported being fairly happy together. But then the Sexual Revolution came along and people said, "We don't need marriage anymore. Anyone can live together for however long they want to for whatever reason they want to and shouldn't have to be bound together 'till death do us part." We want freedom to express ourselves anyway we choose. We don't need God or the institution of marriage that He created." Then the minority of people who were unhappily married or who grew up in an unhappy home led the rebellion. They took over the legislatures; they took over the judicial system, they took over the entertainment industry and popular culture. They took over the schools, they have told us lie after lie in order to try to convince us that their own immoral behaviors are OK. Since this war on marriage and family began they dragged our culture down deeper and deeper into the gutter. Even though the average American's lifestyle is not like TV shows and movies make it out to be Hollywood continues to portray us that way. They are constantly pushing their immorality on us. The message is clear: If you aren't sexually promiscuous then shame on you. In addition, Hollywood exports this false view of Americans to the rest of the world. One of the major reasons there so many enemies in the Christian, Muslim, Judaism and Asian cultures is that they think we are all a bunch of sex addicts and perverts. They don't realize that most Americans are not like that. I believe one of the gravest mistakes occurred when we lost sight of God's purposes for marriage and sex.

As a result, many people see marriage and sex inside of marriage as too limiting. They say things like, "God is against sex" and "God doesn't want us to have any fun." They don't think that their needs can be met through marriage. They use various alternatives to try to meet those needs on their own. But when we gain a correct view of God's purposes for marriage, only then can we realize how God uses marriage to protect us and provide for us better than any way we can devise on our own. God tells us why He created the institution of marriage. God has at least 5 purposes for marriage and sex that are found in Genesis chapters one and two. The Trinity being first purpose for marriage and sex is to reflect God's oneness. Genesis tells us, "Then God said, 'Let us make man in our image, in our likeness.' "In order to understand oneness that two people can experience in a relationship together we need to understand God who makes that possible. To do that, we'll have to dive right in to some pretty heavy theology. You've learned somewhere that God has three persons yet is one God. Does this mean Christians can't count? Does this mean we believe in three Gods or one God? The doctrine of God's Trinity can be very confusing but once we begin to understand it we see how God experiences the ultimate oneness in relationship. In order to make any sense of this, we have to distinguish between what the one refers to and what the three refers to. The one refers to God's essence or nature, in other words, His Goodness, His Divine essence. No one else in the spiritual or physical universe has the divine essence. Indeed, there cannot be any other because there is no room for any more beings with a divine essence. God's divine essence takes up the whole universe. The divine essence cannot be divided between more than one god; otherwise it is not truly the divine essence. It is not that God is merely characterized by a divine essence; God is the divine essence and the divine essence is God. The three refers to three distinct persons. All the persons of the triune God share the divine essence. There is only one divine essence, but there are three persons who share this same nature. The members of the trinity are distinct (The Father, the Son and the Holy Spirit). Does it sound like I just contradicted myself? I haven't because the difference is this. The gods of mythology are distinct beings that act independently. They each have their own agenda. They are seen scheming against and fighting with each other.

The Purpose for Sex

In 180 degree contrast, the members of the trinity are perfectly and deeply interrelated. They have an unbreakable unity. It is said, "For in the divine life there is no isolation, no insulation, no secretiveness, and no fear of being transparent to another." So while each of the divine persons (Father, Son, and Holy Spirit) fully similarly...We cannot remove one person from this intimate relationship and have the other two remain intact....Because the members of the Trinity share the same essence and mutually indwell one another, they also act as one rather than in isolation from one another. Even though three distinct wills exist within the Trinity, only one will is ultimately expressed, which indicates the deep unity of the Godhead. So we could answer the question, What is God like? By saying, "a triangle," but a triangle isn't personal. Instead, God answers the question with, "I am giving you a marriage relationship not just to know intellectually what I am like but to experience what I am like." What a teacher! In a marriage relationship we can experience the wonder and beauty of being two distinct individuals with two distinct wills being united by sharing the essence of humanness. God wants the marriage relationship to be the earthly, visible, tangible model for this ultimate oneness. God made mankind in such a way that males and females are distinctly different. So when a man and a woman come together they are two distinctly different people with not only personality differences but gender differences as well. When these two distinctly different genders are brought together they begin to reflect God's oneness. Genesis 1:26 - 28 tells us, "Then God said, 'Let us (the triune God) make man in our image, in our likeness...' So God created man in his own image, in the image of God he created him; male and female he created them." An individual, while made in the image of God, cannot reflect God's oneness. A man and a man or a woman and a woman can not reflect God's oneness. Homosexuality cannot reflect God's oneness. Instead, it is a counterfeit because to reflect God's oneness requires a male and a female. Why settle for less than the real thing? We'll talk more about homosexuality later in the next book "Save the Family." Now how does this oneness in relationship protect and provide for us? We are emotional and social creatures. We are made to love and to be loved. We are made for oneness with another person. But this oneness can't happen in one night.

It takes a commitment to be loyal and faithful to only one person. This commitment is called marriage. This oneness doesn't even happen completely on a honeymoon. It takes years of getting to know each other, working together, living together, fighting together, relating together to experience the true depth of that deep oneness that is possible. So through marriage our needs for deep intimacy and emotional connectedness are met better than any other way. I'd better say something brief about celibacy here so I'm not misunderstood. Celibacy is a God-given exception. It is a calling and a choice. Because God calls a person to celibacy He will take care of that person's needs for deep intimacy and emotional connectedness through His relationship with that person. Moving on, tragically, many young people mistakenly assume that just because their parents don't share emotional intimacy then no one, including them, can find it in marriage. It doesn't have to be that way. My fiancée' and I have had our ups and downs but through it all we have come to experience a deep emotional intimacy beyond what we ever thought was possible as we move toward being married. To achieve oneness on our own without God whether inside or outside of marriage, we rob ourselves of what we are made for. God designed marriage to protect us and provide for us. In Genesis we read, "God blessed them and said to them, Be fruitful and increase in number; fill the earth." The second purpose for marriage and sex is to procreate, that is to make babies and thereby keep mankind from becoming extinct. The first purpose is to be productive in the world, plant some seeds that they grow to make an impact in the world. Over the years, a married couple has sex far more often than for the purpose of producing children. If sex was only for procreation, God had to make it enjoyable so that we would want to do it more often than just for children. Procreation multiplies a godly heritage. Part of God's strategic plan is that through this lineage of godly descendants, Satan's evil rebellion would be defeated. You see, according to various passages in the Bible we learn that before the physical universe was created, God created the angels, including Lucifer, whose name meant "bearer of light," "Morning Star" He was the most awesome angel there was. He got conceited and led a third of all the angels in a coup attempt to replace God as the ultimate ruler of the universe.

The Purpose for Sex

If he had really understood God he wouldn't have tried such a foolish and futile act. Instead of locking them up in prison or wiping them out of their very existence, God formulated a plan. Remember, Lucifer, who is now called Satan, meaning the adversary or opponent, isn't like God. He doesn't know the future and can't figure out God's plan. He may not know any more about God's plan than we know, and that's reassuring. Anyway, part of God's strategy for dealing with this rebellion was to create the physical universe and planet earth and particularly mankind. God simply hasn't given us enough information to completely understand how this is important to His strategy but He isn't obligated to inform us or Satan of His battle plans. One thing is for sure, Satan hates God and anything that reminds him of God. It just so happened that God created mankind in his image, that is, to be finite replicas of the infinite God. So every time a new human being is conceived in its mother's womb there is another replica of God. So God told us to fill the earth with images of Him. Can you imagine anything else that would drive Satan crazier than to turn every corner and see a reminder of the very God he hates? God made humans to be uniquely different than all other living things. Angels cannot reproduce and make more angels. And while sexual reproduction is important to all living creatures it is given a cosmic significance when it comes to human reproduction. When humans have sex to make babies it takes on the most mysterious meaning of making other humans that bear God's image. This is why abortion is wrong. It treats a human baby like the flesh of any other animal when instead it is a person that bears God's image. It delights Satan when babies are killed because then he doesn't have to risk the possibly of them growing up to become Christians and joining the fight against him. There is yet another reason God gave us sex and that is, to teach us to give unselfishly to one another. God endowed men and women with certain anatomical parts that produce pleasure but are not necessary for intercourse and procreation. Humans have the ability to prolong sex and to give and receive mutual pleasure. We can express love and affection by giving pleasure to our mate that goes way beyond what is necessary to simply make babies. Both marriage partners enjoy sex more when they learn to give and receive this extra pleasure. Their relationship is enriched and deepened as they learn to give to each other.

The Kingdom Culture Community

Genesis 1:26 tells us, God blessed them and said to them, "Be fruitful and increase in number; fill the earth and subdue it. Rule over the fish of the sea and the birds of the air and over every living creature that moves on the ground." Lions are not the king of the beasts, humans are. Even though God built many self-managing checks and balances into nature He put mankind in charge of nature. Instead of managing His creation Himself, God chose to delegate the task to mankind. What a responsibility! In chapter 2 of Genesis we learn that man was created to be a steward of the land. Even before Adam sinned God put him in the Garden of Eden "to work it and take care of it." (Gen. 2:15) As wonderful as the description of the Garden sounds it was not self-maintaining. This shows us that work is not the result of Adam's sin. The part of the curse involving work seems to deal with the frustration we feel when we work. Work is something God created us to do in order to manage His creation. Now, once we understand how special God's creation is and what kind of responsibility we have to be good managers of it, we realize we must work together effectively and constantly depend on God for wisdom and strength. The family unit is uniquely designed to manage God's creation. When we are working together as a family unit we experience God's protection against the hostilities of nature and He provides us with the food and resources we need to live. Inevitably, the picture that comes to mind is a farming family. The husband is out plowing the fields and doing manly work. The wife is cooking, cleaning, canning fruits and vegetables, knitting clothes and doing things for the children. She's doing the "woman's work." But most of us don't live on a farm. So how are we to apply this business of managing God's creation together if we don't deal directly with the land? There are more gender differences than just physical strength. And the gender differences run so much deeper than merely who has to do the cooking and cleaning and take out the trash. Males and females think differently, approach problems differently, feel differently, etc. Paul says" For the husband is the head of the wife as Christ is the head of the church, his body, of which he is our Savior. Now as the church submits to Christ, so also wives should submit to their husbands in everything."" Husbands, love your wives, just as Christ loved the church and gave himself up for her to make her holy,

The Purpose for Sex

cleansing her by the washing with water through the word, and to present her to himself as a radiant church, without stain or wrinkle or any other blemish, but holy and blameless. In this same way, husbands ought to love their wives as their own bodies. He who loves his wife loves himself. After all, no one ever hated his own body, but he feeds and cares for it, just as Christ does the church for we are members of his body. For this reason a man will leave his father and mother and be united to his wife, and the two will become one flesh. This is a profound mystery, but I am talking about Christ and the church. However, each one of you also must love his wife as he loves himself, and the wife must respect her husband." When a husband loves his wife with the selfless, unconditional, sacrificial and trustworthy love with which Christ loves us and the church, his wife normally should have no problem at all submitting to him. If she can't, she needs to examine her own self to find out why. Finally, it is the husband's mission in their marriage to lead her to more spiritual maturity so that she reflects God's character more and more beautifully. So the marriage relationship is to serve as a model of the church's relationship with Christ, while the church's relationship with Christ serves as a model for the marriage relationship. This is truly an amazing, beautiful thing and an incredibly powerful weapon against Satan and his rebellious forces.

CHAPTER V
The Purpose for The Family

What Is Family? In our contemporary Western society, a family is a socially recognizable group. One obvious sign of a family is that of a common residence, housing "two or more persons related by birth, marriage, or adoption, who reside together" (U.S. Bureau of the Census definition). In addition, there is usually a long term commitment of the man and the woman, a joint economic goal, other shared goals and values, a socially approved relationship, and natural and/or adopted children. The primary function of a family is that of reproducing society, which also includes reproducing the concept of family, even among those who don't have children. The historical and traditional assumption in the socially approved concept of family is that it is an institution that exists as being essential for the continuation of creating life within a protective society, which goal cannot be realized without the birth, nurture, training and education of the children. The family also ensures the survival of the family members by providing the protective aspect of the instinct in human life which provides safety of the family. This security also promotes sharing work and property, mutual emotional support, and the birth, growth and nurturing of children. The head of the household is now seen as more of a shared responsibility assumed by the man and the woman, or siblings, if that's the case. A single parent is the sole head of the household. Within this family unit, children have an environment in which they have favorable physical, social and emotional development within acceptable social norms. Single parent families, however, are at a tremendous disadvantage because of the lack of observable male and female gender roles by children in the family. The same may be said of families where siblings are the heads of the household.

A functional family will demonstrate involvement in mutual activities, and a standard of acceptable behavior, defined and stated by the head(s) of the household. There will also be various types of dialogs engaged in, some conflict between various members of the family. However, there is usually a dedication based upon family loyalty that will override differences that may be observed. A healthy functional family will elevate communication to a dialog, wherein there is a mutual exchange of thoughts. The honest exchange of ideas and emotional feelings will, of course, be within the family. However, there will also be an exchange with others who are outside of the immediate family. As parents continue to exchange dialog with each other as a man and a woman, and their sons and daughters, they will exhibit their different gender personalities and characteristics. This gives their sons and daughters an appropriate role model to evaluate. Arguments that occur must be within the broad construct of appropriate male and female sexual gender roles of the parents accompanied by problem solving skills that their children will learn to identify their own sexuality and their own independent and personal identity. Within this area it's important for Mom and Dad to be Mom and Dad and for their children to be sons and daughters with mutual trust earned by each. When those involved step outside of their actual relationships to each other, for whatever reason, the result is emotional and mental chaos. Mom and Dad will be seen by the children as dependable in their financial and emotional support of their children. The children will not be assigned parental responsibilities. Rules will be consistently fair to all but still allow for some flexibility when needed. All functional families will go through times of dysfunction because of death in the family, loss of employment by the family members of the household, serious sickness, emotional problems, and other stress factors. The functional family, however, will return to its norm after the crisis has been resolved. It's important to understand that arguments will occur. However, the healthy functioning family can use those very differences of opinions to develop individual problem solving skills. The family members will learn to talk about their problems, both within and outside of the family, in an honest and open manner. Learn to recognize boundaries and expectations in problem-solving methods.

The Purpose for the Family

The solution will tend to eliminate the tendency towards blame and resentment. Parents will be parents, but they will continue to change and adapt as they for flexibility reasons teach their children how to develop into men and women who may someday be parents to their families. A dysfunctional family is one in which the relationships between the parents and/or children are strained and unnatural. When the traditional cultural concepts of what a man is and of what a woman is, are counterfeited, then the family fails to achieve its intended Kingdom Cultural purpose. This can be a contributing cause of emotional dishonesty, conflict, misbehavior, shame based relationships, and abuse. It's by observing the role modeling of their parent's different genders during their formative childhood years that children learn their emotional responses and gender behavior for their own selves. Throughout the history of mankind the families in society are so obvious and detailed so as to make observations about it unnecessary. Much has changed historically, however, so the descriptions of a contemporary family in today's society must reflect what is lived as Godly principle today. The biggest change we see arguably is that the head of the household is now seen as more of a shared responsibility assumed by the man and the woman. Also the accelerated divorce rate prevalent today, with the average American marriage lasting lest than seven years, the primary cause being the "your-fault" concept. This high divorce rate effectively undermines the purpose of the primary function of the family concept in creating and nourishing life within a controlled society. This has resulted in a weakening of the institution of marriage, with attendant losses in moral, spiritual, personal and public areas of the Kingdom life. The devastating effect upon children who grow up to be parents themselves are full of psychological dangers and undesirable behavior that further promote unhealthy social practices. The attempt to prevent divorce by simply not getting married and then pretending that everything is "just fine" for living and raising children is self-defeating. One cannot really fool one's conscience the way one may practice a mass abortions. This irresponsible behavior has also opened up the door for politicians to jump on the "theory of same-sex marriages" in order to garner votes for themselves in order to continue to "follow the money." The question is: "What kind of values does one really want to practice and preserve for one self and their children's, children?"

The Kingdom Culture Community

The Family of God, the relationship of the disciple of Jesus Christ to our Heavenly Father is sealed by son ship (Romans 8:14, 19), adoption (Romans 8:15, 23; 9:4; Galatians 4:5; Ephesians 1:5) and marriage (John 3:29; Revelation 19:7, 9; 21:2, 9; 22:17) into His family. God is our heavenly Father, Jesus is our Savior and Messiah and believers are brothers and sisters. That makes us the family of Christ. In the New Testament, the family members, both Jew and gentiles grafted into the true Israel met daily, primarily in homes, and centered their activities around prayer, teaching of God's truth and a shared meal. Meetings in the homes, and the new converts soon found that their new lifestyle, free of idolatry, incest, adultery and pagan practices and beliefs was liberating. In this liberating spiritual climate, there was a conscious awareness of acknowledging and worshipping Jesus as the Son of the true and living God and the one true Shepherd to whom they were accountable, instead of their images and idols "Consider one another" ... consider what? "To provoke unto love and to good works:" Why do we assemble together? "... exhorting one another: and so much the more, as ye see the day approaching." The focus is upon "one another." We edify "one another" according to scriptural values, not the traditions of men. Paul is saying to the Corinthians that on those occasions whenever you happen to meet together, then "every one of you have a psalm, have a doctrine, have a tongue, have a revelation, have an interpretation. Let all things be done to edifying." There is no planned meeting at a certain time, on a certain day, for a certain reason. He is saying that whenever you happen to meet together, that the dissension gifts of the Holy Spirit will become operative in the lives of those believers who are in attendance. That could easily be those two or three who happen to meet at a restaurant, or at a mall, or drop by to say hello, or any number of places. The eternal purpose of God was being realized in these various local assemblies, polarized in unity around the truth of God, bound together in love, reproducing in image and likeness of Jesus, and fellowshipping in the true sense of the word. They shared what they had with those who didn't have. They socialized through meeting daily. Eventually, with the passage of time, the newness and excitement of their new found faith faded and they began to meet weekly. They supported those who needed food, clothing, shelter, medical care, transportation and loving family relationships.

The Purpose for the Family

Apostles and prophets were building up elders and deacons in those local assemblies. Evangelists were being sent out, the dynamics of wholesome growth and expansion was set in motion. Those who are disciples of Jesus Christ, learned of Him, followed Him, supported Him and recognized Him as the only true Shepherd to whom they are accountable. These Christian families simply meet together as a family, as the Holy Spirit led them, not on some regulated basis, in order to focus on "one another." But focus on one another and recognize Jesus as their only spiritual head which would automatically prompt worship of Him as stated in scripture. Just Christian families meeting together as a family, focused on "one another" and recognizing and being led by the Holy Spirit through the Glory of Jesus Christ! The family of God is lacking the true function and purpose for which they were created; it is hard for them to favorably influence those with whom they have to do who don't know Jesus Christ as their personal Savior? House churches are a weak solution, when the saints attempt to bring the institutional church system into their living rooms when they are simply perpetuating the system. Do you invite your family over and then arrange chairs all lined up to face a podium so someone can lecture them for an hour or two? And not permit honest, open dialog about the issues of life? How is spiritual truths practice? How is GOD implemented? (If you do not know, you have a real problem!) Do you really want to nourish, reproduce and perpetuate the concept of an institution, organization or a corporation instead of a Kingdom family? More precisely, your choice is to reproduce a true family of God not a dysfunctional family, the sinner man produce enough dysfunctional families. The divine purpose for the family's existence is when God created mankind; He created them as male and female, bringing man and woman together with specific purposes. Adam and Eve were commanded to be fruitful and multiply, to fill and rule the earth (Gen. 1:26-28; 2:7-8, 15; 21-25). Adam's rule began with cultivating the garden that God planted. Beyond these stated purposes are two significant reasons for their existence. First, they were to meet each other's needs for companionship. God did not create man to live alone -- He created them male and female, and it was not good for man to be without his counterpart. Second, they were created to have fellowship with God and to walk with Him.

Therefore, we can summarize the primary purpose for family in the following manner: to glorify God by ruling over God's creation, while enjoying intimacy with one another and with God Himself. This dominion would take place as the couple reproduced a godly heritage and literally filled the earth. This purpose would be fulfilled as a family. Because of the fall into sin, intimacy between God and man, as well as between the man and woman, would be marred and difficult because of the sinful nature. Man failed to rule God's creation in the sense of caring for and administrating it faithfully and wisely. Sons were born after man's image (Gen. 5:3) and a godly heritage was not produced. As God's plan of redemption unfolds, one sees His new plans for mankind. What are these "revised purposes" for the family? Even though mankind has strayed from God's original plan for creation, it can be shown that His purposes for the family (from the sinful fall until the new heavens and new earth) continue to relate to that original plan in Genesis 2. There are several perspectives to focus upon: the family exists in order to provide for basic human needs. God designed the family to be the primary context in which the basic human need of companionship could be met. Man was created with a need for human relationships (Gen. 2:18), and he was told to cleave to his wife (2:24). Parents provide for physical needs of children (Prov. 31:15, 27; 1 Thess. 2:7). The closeness of the family is seen throughout Scripture, from the story of the patriarchs through the record of the early church. One example is the nation of Israel camping and traveling together as families (Num. 2:2; 3:4). Although the family unit must not become self-focused by neglecting "strangers," widows, orphans, and others in the community who do not have a family (Lev. 19:10, 33-34; Prov. 31:20; Mat. 25:35-40; James 1:27), a main purpose for the existence of the family unit is to provide for the physical, emotional, and spiritual needs of its members. (Care for extended family members is expressed in passages like Lev. 25:25; Gen. 29:14; Deut. 25:5-10.)The importance of caring for one's own family is seen in the qualifications for church leadership: elders and deacons had to be good managers of their homes, raising their children well (1 Tim. 2:4, 5, 12; Titus 1:6). This importance is also seen in the emphasis given to the woman's commitment to the home (1 Tim. 2:15; 5:14, 16; Titus 2:4-5).

The Purpose for the Family

In the 1 Timothy 5:16 passage, Paul says the family has the primary responsibility for caring for "dependent widows" -- the church ministers to widows without families. Spiritual care and training are implied in the texts relating to the woman's role (Prov. 31; 1 Tim. 5:14), and the man's role (1 Tim. 3:4-5; 1 Thess. 2:11), but this spiritual training deserves special attention. The husband-wife and parent-child relationship are designed to provide a place where spiritual life is nurtured, tested, and lived for the glory of God. God preserved Noah's family as a godly remnant, and after the flood the family received God's commission to be fruitful and multiply and fill the earth; then they built an altar and worshipped God (Gen. 8:16--9:1). Joshua and his family chose to serve Jehovah (Jos. 24:15). Festivals and feasts were to be celebrated together within the family (Ex. 12:3-14) and these events were to serve as visual reminders and "teaching tools" for future generations (vv.26-27). The commandments and laws were to be taught by the parents to the children -- in the home and within the day-to-day activities of normal family life -- and these instructions were also to be clear reminders of God's redemptive power and purpose (Deut. 6). Since God determined that the primary location for this instruction to take place would be within the family context, one finds multiple instructions in Proverbs regarding the parent-child relationship. Before discussing this spiritual education of children in more detail, it is necessary to reflect on God's purpose for the marriage relationship. It brings honor to God for a man and his wife to cleave to each other, to enjoy the one flesh relationship without shame (Gen. 2:24; Prov. 5:15-19, Heb. 13:4), and to not be separated by divorce (Mark 10:9). The commitment to the marriage is underscored by the seventh commandment, forbidding adultery, and the tenth commandment, forbidding coveting of one's neighbor's wife. In the marriage relationship the man and woman meet each other's physical needs (1 Cor. 7:1-7), as well as emotional and spiritual needs (Eph. 5:22-33; 1 Pet. 3:1-7). The Ephesians passage shows something else about the purpose of marriage, although stated indirectly: since the relationship between man and wife pictures Christ and the Church, somehow this institution, when characterized by love and submission, exemplifies Christ's love for and relationship to the Church.

(This unconditional, sacrificial love of God was also illustrated by Hosea's taking, and remaining faithful to, an unfaithful wife.) There is also an additional purpose implied in the marriage relationship. Since God created man in His image, male and female, there exists the possibility of man and woman knowing God better through the intimate communion and communication between them: as they discover new things about their mate, they get to know a little more about their Creator. In this environment of love and faithfulness, the parents can accomplish God's will in the home (Col. 3:18-21). It is clear from Psalm 127; 128 that having children is a blessing from God. As stated earlier, parents have primary responsibility for the physical care and moral development of their children. Children are repeatedly commanded to honor their parents (Ex. 20:12, Eph. 6:2). Jesus himself set an example in His home life by being subjected to His parents (Luke 2:51). Parents are commanded to train the children with God's values, while maintaining a good balance in loving discipline in order to prevent the child from developing a negative disposition (Eph. 6:3). There are many poor examples of parents who failed to raise their children in the "discipline and admonition of the Lord," such as Eli, Samuel, and David. These examples indicate that the family is crucial -- the failure of the fathers is clearly noted by the Scriptures. The man's leadership in the home may also be in view as whole households sometimes came to faith (Acts 18:8). Hospitality is an important theme in the Scriptures. It is so significant that church leaders had to be hospitable (1 Tim. 3:2), and we are told to show hospitality to strangers (1 Tim. 5:10; Heb. 13:2) and to one another (Rom. 12:13) -- and to do so without complaining (1 Pet. 4:9)! The Lord and His disciples were dependent on people opening their homes to them (Mat. 10:11-14), and some homes, such as Mary and Martha's, were continually opened to the Lord (Luke 10:38). The early church also met in homes (Acts 2:46; 20:20; 1 Cor. 16:15, 19; Rom. 16:5, 23; Col. 4:15). The family that has its own physical and spiritual needs met, through mutual love, is in the best position to open its home and minister to others! Paul's teaching on the husband wife relationship is a pattern of the bride's (Church) relationship to Christ (Ephesians 5). Paul makes this compelling connection in Ephesians 5:32.

The Purpose for the Family

After discussing the couple's responsibility toward each other, He quotes Genesis 2 (leaving and cleaving to become one flesh) and says, "This is a great mystery, but I speak concerning Christ and the church." The familial relationships are used multiple times in Scripture to transmit essential truths; the idea is understood because of the common appreciation for the illustrations. Two examples are Paul's reference to his care for the church as a nursing mother and a committed father (1 Thessalonians 2), and our Lord's encouragement to confident prayer based on how a father treats his children (Matthew 6:7-11).God's broad, eternal purposes in creation and redemption certainly include the family! Scripture has much to say about families, homes, marriages, and the parent-child relationship; it appears that we can summarize the purposes for this institution within the illustrations above. God is glorified as the family provides for each other's basic needs, realizes spiritual nurture, establishes an environment where ministry to others can be accomplished, and functions as a visible example to teach spiritual truth. Family life is a system of human relationships designed by God to provide man's needs. In the family, man finds companionship, sexual satisfaction, and learns love, which is an attribute of God himself. It is in the family that children learn to become socialized. No other arrangement has ever been devised as a successful alternative. It is evident that Jesus was serious when he said, "Therefore what God has joined together let not man put separate" (Matthew 19:6). That which God has provided, ordained, and authorized has always been a focus of attack by the forces of Satan. Today, the family system of life is a major issue in the Devil's warfare against God's design for a fulfilling human relationship. Many couples are asking themselves what is missing in their relationship with one another. Why don't parents really feel close to their children? Why doesn't the family have that warm, close feeling that families should have? Could anything change the situation and bring the joy back into family life? Increasingly, these are the questions being asked by all segments of our society, and for good reasons. For example, there is evidence that negative, unhappy family life is associated with mental health problems and juvenile delinquency. There is a higher incidence of divorce and marital unhappiness among persons who are reared in unhappy families. The challenge of strengthening family life depends upon gaining knowledge about strong, healthy families.

The Kingdom Culture Community

We might ask what we can learn from strong, healthy families that can be applied to our own family to strengthen it. Studies have demonstrated that strong families are characterized by various qualities. An outstanding example of the expression of appreciation is found in the Apostle Paul's letter to the Thessalonians. The first chapter of I Thessalonians is a hymn of praise and thanksgiving for the faith, love and. steadfastness of the Thessalonians. Paul certainly expressed his appreciation for these members of the family of God. An outstanding characteristic of strong families is the great amount of time they spend together. They work and play together. They enjoy being together, even if they are not doing anything in particular. Life today has become very much a "rat race". Family living can be improved by not allowing our lives to become overly fragmented. Strong families intentionally cut down on the number of outside activities and involvement's in order to minimize fragmentation of their family life. When you find yourself becoming so busy that you are not spending time with your family, it is time to look at what you're doing that's taking you away from your family. You may find that some of those involvements are not so important after all. Men should fight to keep your family "number one" in terms of how you spend your time. Strong families spend a lot of time in family discussion and in talking out problems as they come up. There are quarrels in every family, but by getting things out in the open and talking about them, the problem can usually be identified and the best alternative for resolving the conflict can be chosen. Successful marriages and family relationships are characterized by positive, open channels of communication. It is not just communication which contributes to the strength of a family, but communication of a positive nature, marked by a frequent expression of appreciation toward each other. The fourth characteristic of a strong family is a high degree of religious orientation. In addition to attending church as a family, the members pray together and read the Bible and other inspirational books together. The role that religion plays in strengthening families is much more than simply participating in religious activities. It is the knowledge that God is with you every day and is directing your life. Knowing God cares is the greatest friend you have, and has a purpose for your life is a great comfort. The awareness of God's love makes the family more tolerant and forgiving.

The Purpose for the Family

Christianity emphasizes values such as commitment, respect, and responsibilities for the needs and welfare of others. These values contribute to good interpersonal and family relationships. Commitment is the fifth quality of a strong family. A strong family is committed to helping and making each other happy. Their actions are geared toward promoting each other's welfare. Time and energy are invested in the family. Individual goals are frequently sacrificed for the welfare of the family. Strengthening your family can be challenging but these illustrations help you: Develop the art of expressing sincere appreciation to your spouse and children. Concentrate on their individual strengths. Arrange to spend more time with your family. Plan more family activities that all find enjoyable. Learn to say "no" to outside demands which aren't really that important anyway. Open the communication channels. Take time to talk with each other often and be a good listener. Explore ways that spiritual strength might be added to your family life. Participating in church activities as a family, reading religious materials and family devotionals are only a few of the ways this might be accomplished. Build a high degree of commitment toward your family. Make family life your number one priority. Invest your time and energy into the relationships with your spouse and children. The result can, and will be a stronger, more fulfilling Family Life!

Part II:

GODS Foundation

CHAPTER VI

600 Million

The average volume of semen produced in a single release varies from 2 to 5 ml. The semen from a single release may contain between 40 million and 600 million sperm, depending on the volume of the release. Men with normal sperm counts can increase their chances of fathering a child through sexual relationships. A recent medical article shows that men with low sperm counts can increase their chances of fathering a child through extreme sexual relations. Ten to fifteen percent of couples are unable to have children. In more than 40% of marriages, a defect in male sperm is the cause. The normal release contains between 50 and 600 million sperm. Men who produce fewer than 50 million sperms often are infertile. Therefore, higher sperm counts increase a man's chances of fathering a child. A woman releases an egg once every 28 days and is fertile for only about 3 days a month. Twenty-four hours after she releases an egg, her body temperature rises 1 1/2 a degrees. So a woman can take her early morning temperature and try to become pregnant on the morning of/ or before/ her body temperature rises. On the first try, normal men usually produce more than 600 million sperm. A second try 20 minutes later produces 120 million sperm. A third tries 6 hours later produces 10 million, and a fourth 24 hours later makes only 200,000. The latest research shows that men with low sperm counts do not reduce their sperm counts with consecutive releases. So, they could try to make love as often as possible when a woman releases an egg /or doctors can collect successive release and insert them together into the. The 200 - 600 million sperm normally found in a release, increases the chance that some will reach a mature egg, eventually with just one being able to enter and fertilize it. Evolution likely accounts for the high sperm count in a typical releases — a male who is able to produce more sperm obviously has a better likelihood of fertilizing a female than his competitors. In some species, this male may be the one with the largest testicles, which produce more sperm than smaller size.

So, what happens to most of the released sperm on their journey to the egg? Well, as sperm swim through the vaginal canal and into the cervix, they hit a "fork in the road," so to speak. At this juncture, some sperm travel to one fallopian tube, while the rest move on to the other. However, only one fallopian tube has a fertile egg at a given time. The sperm that do not reach an "impasse" surround the mature egg and compete with the other sperm in trying to penetrate it. If a woman's sexual and reproductive health is in good working condition, the first sperm to cross the finish line (enter the egg) succeeds in fertilizing it. "Helper" sperm can also be credited for easing fertilization by allowing this particular sperm access to and contact with the mature egg during its trip. With conception initiated, the now fertilized egg sets off some mechanisms, such as thickening of cervical mucus and hardening of its outer surface (zonapellucida), to block all other sperm from entering the egg. Interestingly, some researchers have theorized that sperm have adapted to take on certain roles, other than for fertilization. For example, abnormal sperm that cannot fertilize may instead function to find and destroy or block competing sperm from other males that also may be making the rounds through a female's reproductive tract. This hypothesis is not without controversy. Alternatively, other researchers have argued that abnormal sperm are simply abnormal. Regardless, it's agreed that more research needs to be done on sperm structure and function before greater consensus can be made. Studies show that one in every seven couples wishing to conceive is infertile. Earlier, it used to be assumed that the problem was solely due to disorders in the woman's reproductive system. However, it is now generally recognized in medical circles that 35-40% cases have male contributing factors. This is quite incredible considering an average, healthy male releases around 120 – 600 million sperm each time he releases. Reproduction should be easy for the male......but sometimes, things go a bit awry. Male infertility could be on account of congenital disorders or could be acquired at any time during his reproductive years and usually has to do with sperm abnormalities such as low sperm count, insufficient motility and abnormal morphology. So what is it purpose for this entire segment? Here is the purpose within 600 million sperms traveling through woman's reproductive system and in this system there are two eggs within her fallopian tube to reach the uterus.

600 Million

Out of 600 Million Sperms fighting for position and only one single sperm is able to enter in one of the eggs. Once entering that egg the most powerful expression of the right hand of GOD take place called "The Germination Process," which through that entire process comes to YOU! GOD chose you out of 600 Million Sperms to be the one to enter this world with powerful skills and abilities He place in you that His purpose and plan can be carried out. SO YOU WERE CHOSEN OUT OF 600 MILLION SPERMS AND YOU STILL DON'T KNOW WHY YOU ARE HERE?

CHAPTER VII

Why Are You Here?

In the beginning, God made the heavens and the earth, day and night, and all the animals on our planet - for a purpose. However, did He create man as some kind of hobby? Have you ever wondered WHY you were born? Does our existence END at death? What is our ultimate destiny? Do we exist to rule the UNIVERSE? The culmination of all creation was to make us "Then God said, 'Let Us make man in Our image, according to Our likeness; let them have dominion over the fish of the sea, over the birds of the air, and over the cattle, over all the earth and over every creeping thing that creeps on the earth. Genesis 1:26. The Hebrew word for God is Elohim, which is a plural form, and for that reason, we find the One who is the Creator referring to "our" image. Amazingly, God consists of more than one being. As the Bible continues its revelation of these Beings, it shows them in a family relationship. Was Adam immortal? Human beings were created in the divine likeness (verse 27), yet physical. When Adam took his first breath, he became a living being. He did not become an immortal spirit on the same level as God, for Ezekiel 18:4 tells us: "Behold, all souls are Mine . . . The soul who sins shall die." (Ezekiel 18:4). The Hebrew word translated as "soul" is "nephesh" which is also used in reference to animals but translated as "creature" in Genesis 1:20, 21, and 24. How could God make man in his own image if he did not give him an immortal spirit? God made Adam to look like himself. He gave him a mind capable of reasoning, thinking, and even creating, although his intellectual powers, in comparison, are limited. Adam came from the dust, the basic element of the earth, which of itself is inorganic or without life. Our Maker had to breathe the breath of life into Adam to make him a fully functioning human. God put Adam and Eve in the Garden of Eden specially designed for them. There were two unique trees in that paradise, a tree of life, and a tree of the knowledge of good and evil (Genesis 2:9).

Notice what the first humans were told: "And the Lord God commanded . . . 'Of every tree of the garden you may freely eat; but of the tree of the knowledge of good and evil you shall not eat, for in the day that you eat of it you shall surely die.' "(Genesis 2:16-17). The implication is that they could have eaten of the tree of life and lived eternally (1000 years). Instead, they chose the other tree and set in motion a world subject to the bondage of corruption, as Paul said in Romans 8:21. As soon as they ate the fruit, they felt different about themselves and their Maker. They were ashamed of their nakedness and wanted to hide from God. Their innocent, trusting relationship with God vanished. They had knowledge of good and evil, but it was not what they expected. Their ultimate punishment was death: ". . . 'For dust you are, and to dust you shall return.' "(Genesis 3:19). God cast Adam and Eve out of the Garden of Eden because of their disobedience and unbelief. They would now have to rest living from a world cursed with thorns and thistles. Humanity had started on the path to destruction. It did not take Adam's children very long to harness the elements to form iron and other metals. They made implements and constructed buildings. They developed a social structure. Left to their own devices, the children of Adam grew so depraved that God had to send a flood to cleanse the earth and start anew with the family of Noah. Because he has allowed us to choose (Our will) our own course, many people do not believe that a divine Creator exists. It is common to hear questions like, "If there is a God, why does He allow crime, war, and disease? If He is truly powerful, why does He not stop these evils? And why does he seem to HIDE Himself ? Many religions teach the separation of man from God due to "the fall." Our creation was perfect and complete; Satan manipulated the mind of Eve which led both Adam and Eve to disregard GODS command, causing a fall from grace. Religion will tell you that God had to come up with some kind of plan to SALVAGE His creation -- a plan to repair the damage. They would have you believe that he has been in a contest with Satan since that time and that the contest continues to this very day. But the Bible says "I form the light and created darkness, I bring prosperity and create disaster; I the Lord, do all these things. Isaiah 45:7. It is important to note that God is in control of Good and Evil! So Satan was a part of GODs plan and purpose which was set before the foundation of the world the scriptures points out.

Why Are You Here

We are GODS greatest achievement, through the human reproductive process He set in motion, God has created countless human beings (regardless of the census stating of 7 Billion people on earth). Moreover, it is His desire that every one of us become complete in His eyes. The Rapture will begin the process when mankind's nature transforms into our complete nature. It is vitally important that we understand how God redeems us. Our salvation is by grace through faith. Christians are His workmanship -- created in Christ Jesus to perform good works (Ephesians. 2:8-10). Many religions would have you believe that there are NO WORKS involved in following Christ. Many Religions teach a person need only accept Jesus to receive salvation. This is not what the Bible teaches! Jesus gave Himself for us:" . . . that He might redeem us from every lawless deed and purify for Himself His own special people, zealous for good works." (Titus. 2:14). The Christian's good works stand as a witness to unbelievers, who will remember them and glorify God in the day of visitation (1Peter 2:12). The plan of salvation will come when Jesus Christ returns to this earth. At that time, He will resurrect those who have died in faith (1 Thessalonians. 4:16-17, Daniel. 12:2-3) and will bring their reward with Him (Revelation. 22:12, Matthew. 16:27). Their reward will be according to their works. (1Cor.10:17). How does a person obtain salvation? What motivates him to want to produce good works and to remain faithful to the end? Before we can walk with God, we must repent. To most people, repentance means being sorry. The Bible, however, reveals much more. In preparing the way for the Messiah, John the Baptist taught the necessity of receiving baptism and bringing forth evidence of repentance (Matthew. 3:8-11). Jesus preached repentance." From that time Jesus began to preach and to say, 'Repent, for the kingdom of heaven is at hand.' "(Matthew. 4:17). Peter cried to the multitudes in Jerusalem gathered to observe the day of Pentecost:" Then Peter said to them, 'Repent, and let every one of you be baptized in the name of Jesus Christ for the remission of sins; and you shall receive the gift of the Holy Spirit. (Acts. 2:38). The first step in salvation is a change of mind, recognition that your ways are not those of the Father, and that your sins have separated you from Him.

Repentance means being sorry for having sinned and having brought about the death of Jesus Christ, who bore the penalty of our sins on the cross."For godly sorrow produces repentance leading to salvation, not to be regretted; but the sorrow of the world produces death. "(2 Corinthians 7:10). The apostle Paul recognized that he had been a blasphemer, a persecutor, and a destroyer. He wrote to his friend Timothy and said: "And I thank Christ Jesus our Lord who has enabled me, because He counted me faithful, putting me into the ministry, although I was formerly a blasphemer, a persecutor . . . but I obtained mercy because I did it ignorantly in unbelief . . . This is a faithful saying and worthy of all acceptance, that Christ Jesus came into the world to save sinners, of whom I am chief." (1Timothy.1:12-13, 15). Despite the sins we did and would commit, God was willing for Paul and all other human beings to be saved and to come to the knowledge of the truth (1Timothy 2:4). He is willing to forgive if we confess our sins and change our lives according to His commandments (Rom.10:9).Once a person has fully repented and been baptized, the Holy Spirit renews his mind (Ephesians. 4:23-24). The Christian becomes a NEW CREATION (2 Corinthians 5:17), who must no longer conform to the values of a world led by the devil. The Citizen of the Kingdom of Heaven must learn to live by God's Word, on Earth:" All Scripture is given by inspiration of God, and is profitable for doctrine, for reproof, for correction, for instruction in righteousness . . ." (2 Timothy 3:16-17). The Bible corrects us and helps us to discern our innermost feelings as they compare to God's way of life. Man has perverted the word of God, polluted his mind, and let his body degenerate. He has failed to train or has wrongly taught his children. He feels resentment and envy - even hatred - toward his neighbor. He tries to get more out of life than he puts in. Yes, why are we special? What potential does GOD see in us? "You have made him a little lower than the angels; you have crowned him with glory and honor, and set him over the works of your hands." Not all things are under our feet just yet. It took Jesus Christ, who as God came in the form of a human, to bring all things into subjection and to taste death for everyone:" For it was fitting for Him, for who are all things and by who are all things, in bringing many sons to glory, to make the captain of their salvation perfect through sufferings."(Hebrews 2:10).

Why Are You Here

The truly converted Citizen of the Kingdom of Heaven becomes a child of God -- a member of a Family first known to man as Elohim. In the beginning, the Family consisted of only two Supreme Beings. Now, it composed of many sons and daughters who will receive eternal life. Jesus is the firstborn of MANY BRETHREN (Romans. 8:29)."Beloved, now we are children of God we shall be like Him, for we shall see Him as He is." (1 John. 3:2).Why did God create us? The purpose of man rests in the plan of salvation and his goal to make man after His own Image. God has reproducing Himself through men and women that He calls a Citizen of the Kingdom of Heaven. When such a person, through baptism, receives the gift of the Holy Spirit, he or she becomes a spiritual son or daughter, though not yet spiritually born again until the confession of (Rom. 10:9). Through Biblical studies day and night, daily prayer, and the experiences and trials of life, the Christian grows spiritually. His human, self-centered nature is reformed and shaped into godly character. Then, at the time of the resurrection, the Christian transforms from mortal to immortal. He is born again. Only this time, he is born into the divine Family, and not into a human family. As he was once born in the image of his human parents, his spiritual birth is the image of GOD. The resurrected Christian will exist and be part of his growing family! This is the wonderful truth why God made us in the first place! May God bless you and give you insight into the meaning and importance of the greatest commandment ever spoken: "Love the Lord your God with all your heart and with all your soul and with all your strength!" (Mark. 12:30)

CHAPTER VIII

The Priest of the Home

In many families, the woman is head of the house, because the man either gave his position up or his position was taken by the woman as foundation of the home. We don't have a submission problem in the home, we have a leadership problem. Many men have decided the woman can be head of man not household. The bible first of all does not say that man is the head of the house hold; the bible says head of the woman. As far as the home the man is the foundation of the home, a home sits on a foundation and everything in it so as for man that is what he was created to be the foundation to handle all things of the world. Remember "Have Dominion Over The Earth"! But because many men haven't been taught how to be that foundation, our society has drawn a picture of men as weaker vessels who allow the woman to instruct them how to run the home. The two roles a man holds in a marriage are that of a priest of the home, and that of being a servant leader. "PRIEST of the Home", men have been called to be the priests in their home. As such, the Old Testament priest serves as an example of what we are to do. There were several things that a priest had to do, that we today, need also to be doing. First of all, a priest had to keep himself undefiled by sin. Since he had to make sacrifices for the people, he couldn't be in a place of sin himself. Every time a priest came on duty, the first thing he did was to make atonement for his own sin, before being in a place to intercede for the people. If the high priest was in sin when he went into the Holy of Holies, he would die. In our families, we must become the example of Christ, "For we are co-workers in God's service; you are God's field, God's building. By the grace God has given me, I laid a foundation as a wise builder, and someone else is building on it. But each one should build with care. For no one can lay any foundation other than the one already laid, which is Jesus Christ." (1 Cor. 3:9-11). As our wives strive to submit, not so much to us but the love in us that we should display not with an "Iron Fist".

We should be so much like Jesus that they are submitting to the love Christ displays to us all. Just as Jesus was without sin, we too must strive to be without sin. In Old Testament worship, one of the main functions of the priesthood was to offer sacrifices for the people's atonement for their sins. They would collect the sacrifices and offerings of the people, and give them to God, keeping the portion for themselves that God had commanded. Fortunately for us; Jesus has made the one and only sacrifice for us. We no longer have to slaughter animals in order to bring the blood before the altar of God. All we have to do is repent and ask for forgiveness, it is already provided. Our children need to see us as willing vessels, quick to repent and ask for God's forgiveness. It is only through our example that they will learn to turn to God, instead of running away from him. Our offerings today are either financial offerings, or time offerings (spending time serving the Lord in the communities). When we neglect to give to God what belongs to God, we are robbing our families of the blessings that He has in store for them. It is God who gives us the ability to gain wealth, that is used to support our families (Deuteronomy. 8:18), none of us are capable of doing it on our own.

Prayer & Intercession
Women tend to be more comfortable praying than men are. For some reason, men tend to leave this area to their wives. However, as priests of the home, the man should be the number one prayer warrior in the family. "But I would have you know, that the head of every man is Christ; and the head of the woman is the man; and the head of Christ is God." (1 Corinthians. 11:3) As head, men are in a unique prayer position. They, and only they, can offer prayer protection and covering to their wives and children. Nobody else is in the unique position to offer that protection. Satan desires to attack and destroy the family; if he can run the priest from the home he can destroy the foundation of the home. But "No man can enter into a strong man's house, and spoil his goods, except he will first bind the strong man; and then he will spoil his house." (Mark. 3:27 & Matthew. 12:29) How does Satan bind you?

The Priest of the World

By keeping you from praying, "For we wrestle not against flesh and blood, but against principalities, against powers, against the rulers of the darkness of this world, against spiritual wickedness in high places." (Ephesians. 6:12) This battle is one that can only be won in prayer. No matter how strong a man is physically, no matter how good a fighter he is in the physical, he can't use that to protect his family. It is only by battling in prayer that men can truly protect their families. Priests are required to become the experts on God's Word. When the people need instruction in God's ways, they are the ones to do it. When the "book of the law" was found in Ezra, it was Ezra, acting as high priest who read it to the people. In our families, it isn't the woman's responsibility to instruct the children about God's ways, it's the woman's responsibility to teach the instruction of the man (Priest/father/husband) as she is instructed (Prov. 1:8-9). Yes, the woman can assist with the instruction, but if the man doesn't take the leading role, the children won't take it seriously. If they don't see their father studying GODS word day and night, they won't read it either. Even if mom studies the Bible regularly, as long as dad doesn't, they will see that they don't have to either. In ancient Israel, it was the man who taught his family the Word of God. Even in more recent times, the Jewish people still have their family worship centered on the role of the father. All of the Jewish festivals, which God established, are celebrated in the home, directed and taught by the father. Paul said "women keep silence in the churches...if they will learn anything, let them ask their husbands at home..." (1 Corinthians. 14:34-35) Part of this was because the Jewish synagogue could be a very noisy place, as they discussed scripture, seeking to understand. Since the women and men sat separately, it would cause a disturbance for a woman to ask her husband a question across the room. However, Paul also makes it clear that a woman is to ask her husband, learning from him not Pastor, Preacher and Teacher over him who stands strong in his position of Priest in the home.

MEN AS LEADERS, God has given the responsibility of being the foundation of the home. I stress the word "responsibility" there because men have a job to do, which they are held accountable to and will have to answer to God for. Anyone who truly knows anything about leadership knows that people don't care how much you know until they know much you care. Leadership begins with the heart, not the head. It flourishes with a meaningful relationship, not more regulation. What is Leadership? Leadership is the process of influencing others. A Leadership principle is "He who thinks he is leading and has no one following him is only taking a walk. Leadership is the ability to obtain followers. In business, that goal may include making a profit, satisfying the customer, or having the best product in the market. In a family, the goal is serving God by way of the Great Commission (Matt. 28 ;) and raising our children. A true leader is a servant. Jesus, while celebrating the last Passover meal with his 12 chosen disciples, took on the role of a servant, and washed their feet (John. 13:4-14). Not only was He carrying out the role as a servant, but the job He chose to do as a servant was usually left for the lowest servant in the house.

To be a leader:

A leader must have Position/Rights know your job description thoroughly.

A leader must have Permission/Relationship possess a genuine love for people.

A leader must have Production/Results Initiate and accept responsibility for growth.

A leader must have People Development/Reproduction realize that people are your most valuable asset.

A leader must have Personhood/Respect your followers are loyal and sacrificial.

The Priest of the World

To lead, you must have an influence. Otherwise, all you are doing is allowing your family to lead by others into a pit. "Where there is no vision, the people perish: but he that keeps the law, he is happy." (Proverbs. 29:18) God has a task for the family, something that He has called us to do, not just us men, but our family as well. God also has a vision for how your family is to function. He's written that plan in his Word. A good leader will study the plan, making sure he understands it, before bringing the plan before his people. You must be sure of the plan, sure of every detail. Otherwise, you can't give adequate direction and guidance. A plan that isn't presented in a clear, definite form won't be followed. There is no reason to follow it, because the leader himself isn't sure where he is headed. As leaders, men are responsible to God for everything that happens in their families. You don't delegate GODS authority given to you as men and you intern gives it to your wife, He won't listen. The Bible says a man apart from his wife his prayers are hindered, (1 Pet. 3:7); you're the one He holds accountable. If your children end up in dangerous sinful ways and means, you must take a peek at the household have they been taught effectively to follow the ways of GOD through Christ Jesus, God won't ask your wife, He'll ask you "BROTHER." If you haven't instructed and taught them effectively in Christ and things go tragically wrong, their blood will be on your hands. Proverbs 22:6 says: "Train up a child in the way he should go: and when he is old, he will not depart from it." It doesn't say he might, it says he will. God has built a training mechanism into us that causes us to return to the ways we learn as a child. The interesting thing is that Proverbs was written to men. Solomon, who was "wiser than all men" (1 Kings 4:31), wrote Proverbs as instruction to his sons. "Hear, O my son, and receive my sayings; and the years of thy life shall be many." (Proverbs. 4: 10) and "Hear, my son, and be wise, and guide your heart in the way." (Proverbs. 23:19) Training of children is the man's responsibility. He can have his wife help, but he is the one accountable to God. Everything that happens in the home is the responsibility of the man.

When there is a problem, it is up to him to find out what the root cause for that problem is, and fix it (dominion over the earth).If the house isn't kept clean, it isn't the woman's fault, it's the man's, and how was your love towards your wife to properly instruct her as to manners of the house (if she doesn't know what to do). Oh, she might be the one who actually does the housework, but it's him that comes along and gives approval to the level of cleaning that's acceptable. If the husband doesn't care, than the wife probably won't do any more than is necessary. But, if he sets a high standard, she'll do everything she can to meet it.

Leaders in Front

To lead requires being out in front. It is impossible to lead from behind. All you can do there is push. When you are trying to lead from behind, you can't maintain the vision or direction. Instead, you end up following those you've put in front. When you stand firm in front, you set the example. Your kids may not always listen to what you say, but you can be sure that they're watching and respect what you do. The same goes for your wife. You can tell her that you expect her to pray and study the Bible, but if you don't she won't. She has been designed by God to be a helper, and will follow in whatever direction you properly lead (under GODLY Principle). When you stand firm out front, you earn respect. Those who are following will look up to you as an example, and desire to have what you have. This gives you the ability to mold and shape things in its proper order, passing on the lessons that you have learned. 1Corinthians. 11:3 says, "But I want you to know that the head of every man is Christ, the head of woman is man, and the head of Christ is God."

The Priest of the World

Prophet

What was a prophet? The word is throughout the Bible and can mean many things. But take it down to its barest essentials: A prophet was someone who had heard something from God. God had spoken His Word to him and revealed His truth to him. A prophet was someone who communicated what he had heard from God to others – specifically, to the people of God. The prophet would spew forth a word of God and like a spring, they nourished and gave life and refreshment. How are we men like prophets? We are to be the ones who, more than anyone else, teach God's Word to our families. Think about it. The pastor only gets one hour a week some two hours to teach God's Word to your family. You get the other 167. Here's the key verse for our prophetic ministry, and it must be a conviction: Ephesians 6:4 says, "And you, fathers, do not provoke your children to wrath, but bring them up in the training and admonition of the Lord." Prophets, practically speaking, need to have a plan for family devotions. I would recommend, if this is something new for you, that you keep it very simple to begin with. Meet for 15 minutes, and the best way to do this is to pick that fifteen minute slot that is going to be the most consistent. For us, that happens to be in the morning, first thing. For some, it may be at bedtime, or at suppertime. But if you pick suppertime, and already 3 of the 7 nights you are not home for supper, you have limited your impact as prophet. Maximize the time. Once you have a time, choose a plan. We have done many different things as a family, and I can make suggestions for you. But here's the bottom line: you need to read some Scripture together. Pick a book you want to take the family through, Dads, and then read a chapter every day. We as prophets to our family need a commitment to disciple our children.

Remember, one of the most important roles of Elijah the prophet, besides speaking the Word of God to Israel was to train the man of God who came after him, Elisha, so that his ministry could be even greater than Elijah's! Remember Ephesians 6:4? "…In the training and admonition of the Lord," Paul said. Again, this must be a conviction. We have to believe that our primary disciples really are our children, and it must be a conviction not a preference, or we will not take it seriously. How do we do this? "Then He appointed twelve, that they might be with Him and that He might send them out to preach." (Mark. 3:14). Our children will be sent out and they will preach what they have been taught and what they have caught from us, from being with us. How do we disciple our children? Spend time going through a book with them, one on one or as a group. Spend time having fun together with your children. We as prophets need the courage to correct and discipline when necessary. Remember this role of the prophet? He would not only communicate what he heard from God, and disciple the ones God had placed under him. He would also correct and discipline when necessary. Nathan confronted King David with his sins. Elijah confronted King Ahab and Queen Jezebel. Paul said we are to bring up our children "in the training and admonition of the Lord." Admonition is a word that means, "To put into the mind." "Proverbs. 29:17 says, "Correct your son, and he will give you rest; yes, he will give delight to your soul." Sometimes my job as Dad means I put something on my child's mind by drawing his attention sharply to another level of her thinking. A priest did two things in the Bible: he went before the people on behalf of God, and he went before God on behalf of the people. The priest goes before the people on behalf of God. What was the indictment of Eli, the priest? His sons committed evil and he did not restrain them. Contrast that with Ezra, another priest in the Old Testament. Ezra 7:28b: "So I was encouraged, as the hand of the Lord my God was upon me; and I gathered leading men of Israel to go up with me." Ezra went before the people to proclaim God's praises, to do and to teach His law, and to hold the people accountable to God's Word as well. Ezra 10:16-19 explains how Ezra dealt with the men in Israel who had married pagan wives.

The Priest of the World

He and the leaders sat down with them. They examined the matter. They asked questions. They found the truth (vs. 18). They saw it through to repentance (vs. 19).Fathers, do you know your children well enough to know if they are pursuing a relationship with the Lord? Do you ever sit down with them and help them, in a loving way, examine their walk with the Lord? Do you ask them questions about their faith and about their walk? When you find inconsistencies, do you stay with it through repentance? This is a crucial responsibility we have as the priests of our own homes. But the sad reality is that many Dads are either too busy pursuing their own lives to invest the time and effort it will take to be a priest to their sons and daughters. Or, they are so caught up in their own foolishness that they have no integrity from which to speak to the foolishness of their children. The priest goes before God on behalf of the people. The priest goes before God on behalf of his people as a worshiper. Who led the worship in the temple? The priests, who was trained and set apart by God to take the people into worship, the priests, who is to be the worship leader in our homes? Dad, who is set apart by God to lead his family into worship? The husband and father who is the worship leader of your family as we gather for corporate worship on Sunday morning? You are! A priest also had to do a lot of work to prepare to take his people into the presence of God. What were all those regulations and ordinances in Leviticus for priests? It was a physical picture of a spiritual reality. Taking people into worship means preparation and responsibility. How much preparation goes into getting your family ready to worship on Sunday morning? The priest goes before God on behalf of the people of God, as an intercessor. Hebrews 7:25 says that Jesus, who is our High Priest forever, always lives to make intercession for them. If Christ is seated beside the Father as our High Priest, forever making intercession for His children, we also are given that great honor and privilege. Pray for your wife. Pray for your children. Bring them before the throne of grace every day, asking the Lord to bless them and to keep them. Get to know what your wife and children are struggling with and pray for them about that.

The Kingdom Culture Community

It is certainly important to pray about the sin we see in our family. And if there is a spiritual attack going on, you have more authority than anyone else in the whole world to deal with it. I ask Lord every morning during early Morning Prayer, "What is your will you call on me to do today Father?" The priest goes before God as a leader, which means we must ask for wisdom concerning the people of God. One of the rebukes of God to the shepherds in Israel was, "My sheep wandered through all the mountains, and on every high hill; yes, my flock was scattered over the whole face of the earth, and no one was seeking or searching for them." (Ezek. 34:6). We must ask for wisdom to know where our family is spiritually. Men! God has put in us from birth a desire to protect. That is standard equipment for men. When a man is protecting his family, it is a picture that makes sense and fits with the reality of God's divine order. When a woman is left to fend for herself or she tries to assume the role as protector of her household, it is a pitiful sight, one that brings shame, one that makes us shake our heads in bewilderment and even disgust. This whole issue of a man as protector of his family goes back to the garden. God created Adam first. He gave Adam His Word: you can eat of any tree in the garden except one. The day you eat of it, you will surely die. Eve was then created to be Adam's helpmeet, and it was clear that God held Adam responsible when he failed to protect Eve from deception. She took of the fruit and ate it, then gave some to Adam, whom, the Bible says, "was there with her." The next thing you know, darkness had fallen on the earth forever and God came calling: "Adam, where are you?" He could have just as easily said, "Adam, where WERE you?" Your wife was deceived, and you were standing right there watching! You were watching it happen and did nothing to stop it, nothing to protect her, nothing to protect your family. Now look what has happened as a result. Remember when Nehemiah was rebuilding the walls in Jerusalem and he was being threatened by Tobias and Sanballat and enemies who threatened to come and attack? What did he do?

The Priest of the World

He stationed the men in front of their own houses to rebuild the wall that, if it were weak, would most compromise the safety of their families. Nehemiah was a wise man. He knew that a healthy fear of attack on a man's own family would be a great motivator for him to build the wall and do it well and not stop until it was done. From what do we protect our family? We protect our family from false doctrine. 2 Corinthian 11:3 say, "But I fear, lest somehow, as the serpent deceived Eve by his craftiness, so your minds may be corrupted from the simplicity that is in Christ." Paul is fearful the church will be deceived – he says in verse 4, by another Jesus, a different spirit, a different gospel. How do we protect our family from false doctrine? By teaching true doctrine! We protect our family from bad companions. Proverbs 13:20 say, "He who walks with wise men will be wise, but the companion of fools will be destroyed." If we are to protect our children, we must be able to recognize when they are attracted to the companionship of a fool. We protect our children from making a lifelong mistake. Young men! There is a mistake you can make that will literally haunt you for the rest of your life. Lots of mistakes are fixable with little consequence, like taking the wrong job, buying the wrong house, even going to the wrong church. But there is nothing to be done for marrying the wrong wife. Men are called to protect their wives from carrying more than they can carry, or even what they should not have to carry at all! Now when you think of being the provider, it may be that your mind goes first to 1Timothy 5:8, "But if anyone does not provide for his own, and especially for those of his household, he has denied the faith and is worse than an unbeliever." However, we must take a wider view of what it means to be a provider. A man provides a vision for his family. You are the visionary for your household, Men! And remember, the very fact that God has brought a helpmate for you is proof that you have a God-sized purpose to fulfill and you cannot do that alone. What is your vision for your family? What do you want to accomplish more than anything else with your children before you let them go towards their own purpose?

The Kingdom Culture Community

These children who are "arrows in the hand of a warrior" (Psalm 127:4). A warrior has a target for every arrow. He lets none fly without taking careful aim. They are so precious. So we should do like Habakkuk suggested and "write the vision; make it plain." I will tell you that my primary vision for my daughter is that she have a growing relationship with Jesus Christ and a love for His Word and His Will. I encourage my daughter have solid, biblical grasp of knowledge, Understanding and Wisdom that she can be counted on to do whatever it takes to help those around her. A man provides for his family's emotional needs. How many of us grew up with Dads who were excellent financial providers but we were starved for affirmation, for approval, for our father's love? The story of Jacob shows that he was an excellent businessman: shrewd, savvy and capable. He amassed a great deal of wealth and his children lived a very comfortable lifestyle, at least until the worldwide famine. But what kind of emotional support did he give his children? Well, not much unless that child's name happened to be Joseph! Jacob played favorites and his other 10 sons (this was before Benjamin came along) got more and more jealous, simply because they had an emotional need for their father's love and approval that was not being met. We know what happened. They sold their brother into slavery! They removed the object of their father's affection. What can happen to a child who is not given what he longs for most, his father's approval? Jacob apparently wasn't much better with providing the emotional needs of his wife. Look at Genesis 29: 30-35 for one of the saddest portions of Scripture related to marriage in the Bible. See that? Leah was a desperate housewife! Because her husband wouldn't give her what she needed: his love. This would be an argument against having more than one wife: no man can give more than one woman what she needs emotionally. But each of us needs to understand this. That's why Peter said to us, "Husbands... dwell with (your wives) with understanding..." (1 Peter 3:7). A man provides for his family's physical needs. There is no question that the biblical teaching is clear. God created Adam, put him in the garden, and told him to tend it and keep it. He gave him a job. Then God created Eve, put her next to her husband, and told Adam that she was his helpmate. The Bible says that I am not my own, that I have been bought with a price, and that my body is the temple of the Holy Spirit. AMEN.

CHAPTER IX

The Inheritance

To understand our inheritance, we must first realize that all of us, as believers in Christ, are priests of God: "But you are a chosen generation, a royal priesthood, an holy nation, a peculiar people; that you should shew forth the praises of him who has called you out of darkness into his marvelous light: Which in time past were not a people, but are now the people of God: which had not obtained mercy, but now have obtained mercy." (1 Peter 2:9-10). We are priests on account that we are God's people now. The Church has grown accustomed to the idea that the only "ministers" or "priests" are those who came out of seminary and hold a full-time position in some well-recognized congregation. This idea, however, grows out of man's carnal desire to create castes among people, but the Lord sees us as One Body, whose members have all been baptized into the same Spirit and into the same Anointing:" For as the body is one, and has many members, and all the members of that one body, being many, are one body: so also is Christ. For by one Spirit are we all baptized into one body, whether we be Jews or Gentiles, whether we be bond or free; and have been all made to drink into one Spirit." (1 Corinthians 12:12-13) "But you have unction from the Holy One, and you know all things." (1 John 2:20).The prophet Isaiah, when speaking about the prophetic manifestation of the Anointed One in Isaiah 61:1-3, says the following a few verses later: "But you shall be named the Priests of the LORD: men shall call you the Ministers of our God: you shall eat the riches of the Gentiles, and in their glory shall you boast yourselves." (Isaiah 61:6). We have been made priests of the Lord, and that we, as believers, shall be called ministers of our God.

Our inheritance as priests, we understand that we all have a priestly calling on our lives, what is our inheritance as priests is supposed to be? "And the LORD spoke to Aaron, you shall have no inheritance in their land, neither shall you have any part among them: I am your part and your inheritance among the children of Israel"(Numbers 18:20). This was what the Lord said to the priests of Israel: "I, Almighty God, am your inheritance". This means that we, as priests, are not to aspire to a temporary inheritance, but rather, we are called to aspire to the greatest inheritance of all: God Himself. This is why the bride says the following to the bridegroom in the Song of Solomon:" I am my beloved's, and my beloved is mine: he feeds among the lilies" (Song of Solomon 6:3). Most believers do accept the fact that the bride in the Song of Solomon is a figure of the Church and that the bridegroom is a figure of the Lord. This means that they must also accept that the bride can dare to say to God that He belongs to her, and there is joy, not anger, in God's heart, when believers understand and believe this in their hearts. He wants you to say to Him, "You belong to me, and I belong to You". Our inheritance, as priests in Christ, therefore, is God Himself. He is the inheritance we are after. He is the reason for our existence and He Himself is our reward. He is the One we are after, and, when we understand that, we enter into our true priestly calling. The nations of the Earth most believers, especially pastors, have misunderstood Who our inheritance really is, and they many times misuse Scripture to fabricate an inheritance that is more appealing to the natural mind, but which removes believers from pursuing their true calling. Before seeing how this "fabrication" is made, "But you shall be named the Priests of the LORD: men shall call you the Ministers of our God: you shall eat the riches of the Gentiles, and in their glory shall you boast yourselves." (Isaiah 61:6). Notice how the last part of the verse speaks about "the riches of the Gentiles". What does this phrase mean? To grasp its underlying meaning, we must go to other passages of Scripture:

The Inheritance

"I will declare the decree: the LORD hath said to me, you are my Son; this day have I begotten you. Ask of me, and I shall give you the heathen for your inheritance, and the uttermost parts of the earth for thy possession. You shall break them with a rod of iron; you shall dash them in pieces like a potter's vessel." (Psalms. 2:7-9).The word translated as "heathen" in verse 8 is the Hebrew word goim, which literally means "nations" or "peoples", so verse 8 should say, "Ask of Me, and I shall give you the nations for your inheritance". The word goim is exactly the same word that is translated as "Gentiles" in the phrase "the riches of the Gentiles" of Isaiah 61:6. This means that our priestly inheritance involves the "nations". To understand how the nations enter into our inheritance, we have to look at verse 9 of Psalms 2, where it declares that we will break the nations with a rod of iron, and dash them to pieces like a potter's vessel. Notice that, when the Holy Spirit speaks to us about inheriting the nations, He does not focus on the enjoyment of their material possessions, but rather about something deeper and much more important, and that is the domination of the spiritual atmosphere of the nations of the Earth. As most believers know, the Bible calls Satan the "prince of the power of the air". "In which you formerly walked according to the course of this world, according to the prince of the power of air, of the spirit that is now working in the sons of disobedience" (Ephesians 2:2). But the Bible also declares that a time will come, when Satan will be cast down from his domination of the spiritual atmosphere on Earth:" Then war broke out in heaven. Michael and his angels fought against the dragon, and the dragon and his angels fought back. But he was not strong enough, and they lost their place in heaven. The great dragon was hurled down—that ancient serpent called the devil, or Satan, who leads the whole world astray. He was hurled to the earth, and his angels with him. Then I heard a loud voice in heaven say: "Now have come the salvation and the power and the kingdom of our God, and the authority of his Messiah. For the accuser of our brothers and sisters, who accuses them before our God day and night, has been hurled down. They triumphed over him by the blood of the Lamb and by the word of their testimony; they did not love their lives so much as to shrink from death.

Therefore rejoice you heavens and you who dwell in them! But woe to the earth and the sea, because the devil has gone down to you! He is filled with fury, because he knows that his time is short." (Revelation 12:7-12). The seventy-two returned with joy and said, "Lord, even the demons submit to us in your name." He replied, "I saw Satan fall like lightning from heaven. I have given you authority to trample on snakes and scorpions and to overcome all the power of the enemy; nothing will harm you. However, do not rejoice that the spirits submit to you, but rejoice that your names are written in heaven." At that time Jesus, full of joy through the Holy Spirit, said, "I praise you, Father, Lord of heaven and earth, because you have hidden these things from the wise and learned, and revealed them to little children. Yes, Father, for this is what you were pleased to do. "All things have been committed to me by my Father. No one knows who the Son is except the Father, and no one knows who the Father is except the Son and those to whom the Son chooses to reveal him." Then he turned to his disciples and said privately, "Blessed are the eyes that see what you see. For I tell you that many prophets and kings wanted to see what you see but did not see it, and to hear what you hear but did not hear it." God will rise up a mighty Church that will, in these latter days, take dominion over the spiritual atmosphere on planet Earth, and He will use those who seem insignificant to men. This is why Jesus says in verse 21 that this spiritual truth will be revealed to "babes" and will be hidden from the "wise and prudent". The mighty remnant that God will raise up is comprised of believers who spiritually live outside the religious structures of the Church. It will not be through the traditionally accepted leadership that is ruling over the Church now, just as it happened in the days of Jesus. It was not through the Pharisees and Sadducees, or through the recognized priests and scribes of the day, that God manifested His Glory. Instead He chose the son of an unknown carpenter's wife and a small group of unknown Galileans, and so it will be in these latter days. In Luke. 10:22 above, Jesus says, "All things are delivered to Me of My Father". Here, again, He is speaking about the spiritual inheritance that the Father has given Him.

The Inheritance

Notice how the whole context around the passage of Luke. 10:17-24 is not about material possessions such as houses and cars but rather about the tearing down of Satan from the air, taking away his title as "prince of the power of the air", and about the manifestation of our spiritual authority in the air. Luke. 10:20 says that we are to rejoice over our names being written in "heaven". This is one of the most misinterpreted verses in Scripture. The Lord here is not talking about our salvation from hell but about the manifestation of our authority. In Scripture, a person's "name" refers to his or her authority and to his or her inner nature. This is why Philippians. 2:10 says that, at Jesus' name, every knee shall bow and every tongue confess that Jesus Christ is Lord. When you received Jesus into your heart, a spiritual star was born in the heavens, in the same way that a literal star appeared in the sky when Jesus was literally born on Earth:" Whereupon are the foundations thereof fastened? Or who laid the corner stone thereof; when the morning stars sang together, and all the sons of God shouted for joy?" (Job. 38:6-7). "The light of the righteous rejoice: but the lamp of the wicked shall be put out." (Proverbs. 13:9) "Light is sown for the righteous, and gladness for the upright in heart. Rejoice in the LORD, you righteous; and give thanks at the remembrance of his holiness." (Psalms. 97:11-12). "Wealth and riches shall be in his house: and his righteousness endures forever. Unto the upright there arise light in the darkness: he is gracious, and full of compassion, and righteous." (Psalms. 112:3-4). "We have also a more sure word of prophecy; whereto you do well that you take heed, as to a light that shine in a dark place, until the day dawn, and the day star arise in your hearts:" (2 Peter. 1:19). "And he shall rule them with a rod of iron; as the vessels of a potter shall they be broken to shivers: even as I received of my Father. And I will give him the morning star." (Revelation. 2:27-28).As your spiritual authority grows, the light of your spiritual star in the heavens grows in intensity, and as that happens, the spiritual forces of darkness are driven out. This means that, as the light of your star grows, the "available space" for the spirits of darkness in the air around you diminishes, until there is no more space for them and they must fall.

The Kingdom Culture Community

Due to the pastoral shield that the Church is currently under, Satan has been allowed to rule the air without major opposition, but, when the pastoral matriarchy is eventually broken, Satan will be driven out of the spiritual atmosphere and will fall. During this time, the greatest revival in human history will take place. This will be the time when the greatest miracles in history will occur, and the Earth (including believers and unbelievers) will, for a few years, live under God's constant judgments. During this time, the Church will rule with a rod of iron, praying for judgments to be unleashed upon all iniquity and evildoing on Earth. During this time, any act of willful sin, inside or outside the Church, will be brought under immediate judgment by a Church of believers that will be constantly praying for judgments. This is why so many will be converted to the Lord during those days: "Now I rejoice, not that you were made sorry, but that you're sorrowed to repentance: for you were made sorry after a godly manner, that you might receive damage by us in nothing. For godly sorrow work repentance to salvation not to be repented of: but the sorrow of the world works death." (2 Corinthians. 7:9-10)

"Whiles it remained, was it not your own? And after it was sold, was it not in your own power? Why have you conceived this thing in your heart? You have not lied to men, but to God. And Ananias hearing these words fell down, and gave up the ghost: and great fear came on all them that heard these things" (Acts. 5:4-5). "For the time is come that judgment must begin at the house of God: and if it first begin at us, what shall the end be of them that obey not the gospel of God? And if the righteous scarcely be saved, where shall the ungodly and the sinner appear?" (1 Peter. 4:17-18).After some years of this spiritual domination of the air, the Bible reveals that a great apostasy will enter the Church, instigated by believers who will be tired of so much judgment and righteousness. Just as the Lord Jesus was betrayed from within, the remnant anointing of the Church will also be betrayed by carnal believers inside the Church, and the remnant's authority will be stricken down. Faithful believers will suffer persecution and rejection for a short time, and those who God will have used to perform mighty signs and wonders will be mocked and ridiculed, but those who persevere until the end will dwell in God forever.

The Inheritance

Therefore since it still remains for some to enter that rest, and since those who formerly had the good news proclaimed to them did not go in because of their disobedience, God again set a certain day, calling it "Today." This he did when a long time later he spoke through David, as in the passage already quoted: "Today, if you hear his voice do not harden your hearts." For if Joshua had given them rest God would not have spoken later about another day. There remains, then, a Sabbath-rest for the people of God; for anyone who enters God's rest also rests from their works, just as God did from his. Let us, therefore, make every effort to enter that rest, so that no one will perish by following their example of disobedience. For the word of God is alive and active. Sharper than any double-edged sword, it penetrates even to dividing soul and spirit, joints and marrow; it judges the thoughts and attitudes of the heart. (Hebrews. 4:6-12). Notice how this passage, which talks about entering into God's rest and about possessing the Promised Land, ends with a reference to the Word of God as a sharp-edged sword that "discerns" the thoughts and the intentions of the heart. The word translated as "discerner" in verse **12** is the Greek word kritikos, which comes from krites, which means, "to judge". In other words, the Church will enter into the rest of God when it begins to apply the word of judgment in the Spirit to execute God's judgments on Earth. This is how the greatest revival in the history of mankind will come, and there is no way around that. And this is how we as believers can enter into the fullness of our inheritance and take over the nations of the Earth and rule them with a rod of iron. A temporary inheritance, in the book of Romans, Paul declares the following:

"**31** What shall we then say to these things? If God be for us, who can be against us? **32** He that spared not his own Son, but delivered him up for us all, how shall he not with him also freely give us all things?" (Romans. 8:31-32).As we mentioned before, most pastors preach on passages such as this one, taking them out of context to give them a purely carnal interpretation. In verse 31, Paul refers to God being for us versus those who might be against us. This means that the passage is talking about conflict and warfare, and as the verses before this passage show, this warfare is not about acquiring bigger houses and fancier cars, but about taking back the Earth to God Rom. 8:17-26:

The Spirit himself testifies with our spirit that we are God's children. **17** Now if we are children, then we are heirs—heirs of God and co-heirs with Christ, if indeed we share in his sufferings in order that we may also share in his glory. **18** I consider that our present sufferings are not worth comparing with the glory that will be revealed in us. **19** For the creation wait in eager expectation for the children of God to be revealed. **20** For the creation was subjected to frustration, not by its own choice, but by the will of the one who subjected it, in hope **21** that the creation itself will be liberated from its bondage to decay and brought into the freedom and glory of the children of God. **22** We know that the whole creation has been groaning as in the pains of childbirth right up to the present time. **23** Not only so, but we ourselves, who have the first fruits of the Spirit, groan inwardly as we wait eagerly for our adoption to sonship, the redemption of our bodies. **24** For in this hope we were saved. But hope that is seen is no hope at all. Who hopes for what they already have? **25** But if we hope for what we do not yet have, we wait for it patiently. **26** In the same way, the Spirit helps us in our weakness. We do not know what we ought to pray for, but the Spirit himself intercedes for us through wordless groans.

Notice how the Holy Spirit relates our inheritance (being "heirs of God" in verse 16) to the restoration of creation, which points once again to the fact that our inheritance involves the spiritual domination of the Earth's atmosphere. Notice also how verse **17** speaks of suffering with Him to be glorified with Him. If our "inheritance" is comprised of getting bigger houses and nicer cars in order to lead a more comfortable life, why would the Spirit speak about suffering in verse 17, about groaning and travailing in verses 22 and 23, and about "infirmities" in verse 26? (By the way, the word translated as "infirmities" in verse 26 is the Greek word asthenia, which is used in Matthew 8:17 to speak about Christ taking our "infirmities" and bearing our sicknesses).Therefore, when Paul talks about God freely giving us "all things" in Romans 8:32, He is not talking about nice cars, big houses, and nice clothes. He is not even talking about good health and happy living!!! He is talking about the "all things" that Jesus spoke about in Luke 10:22 discussed above.

The Inheritance

We are in spiritual warfare, and we are spiritual invaders through whom God will establish His Kingdom on Earth: They have the appearance of horses; they gallop along like cavalry. With a noise like that of chariots they leap over the mountain tops, like a crackling fire consuming stubble, like a mighty army drawn up for battle. At the sight of them, nations are in anguish; every face turns pale. They charge like warriors; they scale walls like soldiers. They all march in line, not swerving from their course. They do not jostle each other; each marches straight ahead. They plunge through defenses without breaking ranks. They rush upon the city; they run along the wall. They climb into the houses; like thieves they enter through the windows. Before them the earth shakes, the heavens tremble, the sun and moon are darkened, and the stars no longer shine. The Lord thunder at the head of his army; his forces are beyond number, and mighty is the army that obeys his command. The day of the Lord is great; it is dreadful. Who can endure it? (Joel 2:4-11).Notice how verse 11 speaks of us as "executers of His Word", Considering that Hebrews 4:12 says that the Word of God judges, we again see how the living out of our calling involves the unleashing of prophetic and apostolic word of judgment into the atmosphere to take it back for God: "To the intent that now to the principalities and powers in heavenly places might be known by the church the manifold wisdom of God, **11** According to the eternal purpose which he purposed in Christ Jesus our Lord: **12** In whom we have boldness and access with confidence by the faith of him. **13** Wherefore I desire that you faint not at my tribulations for you, which is your glory." (Ephesians 3:10-13) When speaking about our inheritance, the Bible constantly associates it with suffering and tribulation, which is very different from the carnal interpretation that is given to the word "inheritance", associating it mostly with comfort and pleasure. This is why, before speaking about our inheritance in Romans 8, the Holy Spirit added the following warning:

"**6** For to be carnally minded is death; but to be spiritually minded is life and peace. 7Because the carnal mind is enmity against God: for it is not subject to the law of God, neither indeed can be. **8** So then they that are in the flesh cannot please God. **9** But you are not in the flesh, but in the Spirit, if so be that the Spirit of God dwells in you. Now if any man has not the Spirit of Christ, he is none of his." (Romans 8:6-9)

When Paul talks about having the "Spirit of Christ" in verse 9, he is not talking about being born again, but rather about having the willingness to suffer just like Christ suffered. That is the only way that the "spirit of the Christ" can abide in us:

"But rejoice, inasmuch as ye are partakers of Christ's sufferings; that, when his glory shall be revealed, ye may be glad also with exceeding joy." (1 Peter 4:13)

"Who now rejoice in my sufferings for you, and fill up that which is behind of the afflictions of Christ in my flesh for his body's sake, which is the church" (Colossians 1:24)

"For as the sufferings of Christ abound in us, so our consolation also abound by Christ" (2 Corinthians 1:5)

What about our temporary needs, then? Paul has the following to say concerning this:

"**11** Not that I speak in respect of want: for I have learned, in whatsoever state I am, therewith to be content. **12** I know both how to be abased, and I know how to abound: everywhere and in all things I am instructed both to be full and to be hungry, both to abound and to suffer need. **13** I can do all things through Christ which strengthened me." (Philippians 4:11-13)

The Inheritance

Our spirit is called to proactively conquer and possess the Earth for the Lord, but our soul is called to be content concerning natural things. Notice how the famous verse, "I can do all things through Christ who strengthens me", comes after speaking about contentment and about being able to endure hardship. Unfortunately, most believers, especially pastors, take verse 13 out of context to justify any endeavor, especially when the endeavor involves making money or the enlargement of a congregation's membership. The "all things" reference takes us back to what we said about Luke. 10:22 and Romans. 8:32. It does not refer to "all my whims and desires"; it refers to the taking of the spiritual atmosphere of the Earth.

To emphasize the "soul contentment" principle, the Holy Spirit says the following:

"**5** Let your conversation be without covetousness; and be content with such things as you have: for he has said, I will never leave you, nor forsake you. **6** So that we may boldly say, The Lord is my helper, and I will not fear what man shall do unto me." (Hebrews 13:5-6) "**6** But godliness with contentment is great gain. **7** For we brought nothing into this world and it is certain we can carry nothing out. **8** And having food and raiment let us be therewith content. **9** But they that will be rich fall into temptation and a snare, and into many foolish and hurtful lusts, which drown men in destruction and perdition." (1Timothy. 6:6-9)

"**31** Therefore take no thought, saying, what shall we eat? Or, What shall we drink? Or, Wherewithal shall we be clothed? **32** (For after all these things do the Gentiles seek:) for your heavenly Father knows that you have need of all these things. **33** But seek first the kingdom of God, and his righteousness; and all these things shall be added unto you. **34** Take therefore no thought for the morrow: for the morrow shall take thought for the things of itself. Sufficient unto the day is the evil thereof." (Matthew. 6:31-34). Paul talks about the riches of His Glory strengthening the inner man by the Spirit (verse 16), and then proceeds to speak about a Church that will fill the spiritual atmosphere of the Earth in Christ. Our inheritance is related to conquering the air, not to making more money.

The Kingdom Culture Community

If you put the establishing of His Kingdom and His justice first, God will provide for your food and covering (clothing and a roof). Possessions on Earth are temporary, and they will only be yours while you live in your earthly body. Go after your eternal inheritance. Don't go after God to get things from Him. That is like a one going after a millionaire because of the money. Go after God because of Him, because of His nature, because you desire Him above all things, and are willing to give everything in you to see His will fulfilled (Matthew 6:10). Your life is not in your car. Your life is in Him:

"Since, then, you have been raised with Christ, set your hearts on things above, where Christ is, seated at the right hand of God. Set your minds on things above, not on earthly things. For you died and your life is now hidden with Christ in God." (Col. 3:1).

A Message To The Family

The family is the most powerful entity in a man's life. The family is a man's life, which carries him through a life of death and destruction that goes on in the world today and beyond. The greatest component that a man can have to overcome all obstacles in life's muck and mire. The greatest way a man can love his children is to love the children's mother, if you are with her or not. It is GOD's primary plan and purpose on earth that the family be successful in staying intact which ultimately represents "The Kingdom of GOD." There is no other survival tactic on earth that is greater than the survival of the family. The greatest attack mechanism that devil has is the attack of the family. If devil can take away the Head/or Foundation/Man/Husband from the home then the demise of the family structure and foundation begins to possible total destruction of the family order GOD intended it to be. Whoever controls the mind controls the body, if devil can remove the man as head/foundation of the family from the house hold, just like the Garden of Eden he can then have dominion over the home as man is to have dominion over the earth. It is vitally important that the man know his responsibilities over the home of the family and not denounce those responsibilities nor hand them over to the Helpmeet/Woman/Wife to carry on with. It is not GODs purpose or plan that the women head the family. MEN you must stand firm out front as the Priest of the home and not allow other spirits and principalities to remove you or regulate your family. Your life depends on it that you know the ways and means of GODs purpose and plan of how the family is to operate in accords to "The Kingdom Culture Community." May GOD always rule in your life through His Son Our Lord and Savior Jesus Christ, Amen.

—ABOUT THE AUTHOR—

In Washington D.C. March of 2008, as the Rev. James Cunningham with over 35 years of Pastoral leadership, was met with great persistence and perseverance from Min. Anthony Martin at that time of knowing such powerful history of him. Once knowing of Rev. James Cunningham great leadership the seed for a church establishment was planted. That seed has been watered well "the bible says one plants...the other waters and...God gives the increase". Two- years later on April 19 2010 the Covenant Church of the Resurrection, Inc was registered in Washington D.C. As an ordained Pastor for over 35 years Rev. Cunningham ordained Min. Anthony Martin as Assistant Pastor. During a 10yr time of his life Rev. Anthony Martin became a community activist performing many volunteering duties in ministry to change many of our youth and adults way of thinking. Performing many of my activity in our local recreations, social organizations and the ministry duties in the field of "Carolina Missionary Baptist, Manifest Sons of God Ministries and Cornerstone Church of God in Christ as a servant of God. In 1996 Rev. Anthony Martin attended and completed Samuel Kelsey Bible Institute for a Bachelors Degree (Master Teachers Studies). Rev. Anthony Martin began the ministry in which God gave him: All Saints Christian Fellowship and Development Ministries that led him back to the fields of labor under Gods direction to uphold his word and to bring souls to Christ. Vision came in the fall of 2008 to bring forth GM Interprise Inc., a non-profit organization to carry out his late great beautiful mothers (Gwendolyn Martin, named of organization) ways and means of being a humbled and powerful servant to the community. He spent much of his life bringing 10 + years business and leadership experience, as a Community Organizer, Community Outreach Coordinator, Motivational Speaker/Teacher, Family Support Worker, ordained Pastor, Founder GM Interprise, Inc., President of GM Enterprise, LLC., Certified Fatherhood Initiative Facilitator of "The Quenching the Father Thirst Program" and "Safe Haven", organized fundraisers. In Dec. 2013 and Jan. 2014 Rev. Anthony Martin became a 5 Time Author of the Books "The Battle of the Culture and "The Kingdom Culture Community", "Stop Killing Me Black Man" and "Stop Killing the Image of GOD and The Foreign Exchange, an Inspirational/Motivational Evangelistic Speaker along with the newly founded ministry "The Kingdom Culture Fellowship Ministries & Christian Self-Publishing Co. Blog Talk Radio Show and coordinated Men's & Woman's Workshops such as "Fulfill A Man's Thirst" & Serve A Woman's Hunger" on a grass roots level in a much needed efforts to continue to "Save the Family".

20 TIME AUTHOR

INSPIRATIONAL/MOTIVATIONAL

EVANGELISTIC SPEAKER

www.ingramcontent.com/pod-product-compliance
Lightning Source LLC
Chambersburg PA
CBHW022106160426
43198CB00008B/377